MANAGING CULTURE

MANAGING WORK AND ORGANIZATIONS SERIES

Edited by Graeme Salaman, Senior Lecturer in the Faculty of Social Sciences and the Open Business School, the Open University.

Current and forthcoming titles include:

Peter Anthony: *Managing Culture*
Michael Armstrong: *Managing Reward Systems*
David Casey: *Managing Learning in Organizations*
Rohan Collier and Susanne Hickmott: *Sexual Harassment in the Workplace*
Patricia Findlay: *Managing Company Employment Policy*
Paul Iles: *Managing Assessment Processes*
Ian McLoughlin and Stephen Gourlay: *Enterprise Without Unions*
John Storey and Keith Sisson: *Managing Human Resources and Industrial Relations*

MANAGING CULTURE

Peter Anthony

Open University Press
Buckingham · Philadelphia

Open University Press
Celtic Court
22 Ballmoor
Buckingham
MK18 1XW

and
1900 Frost Road, Suite 101
Bristol, PA 19007, USA

First Published 1994

Copyright © Peter Anthony 1994

A catalogue record of this book is available from the British Library

ISBN 0 335 09788 X (pb)   0 335 09789 8 (hb)

Library of Congress Cataloging-in-Publication Data
Anthony, Peter.
    Managing culture/Peter Anthony.
      p.   cm. – (Managing work and organizations series)
    Includes bibliographical references and index.
    ISBN 0–335–09789–8 (hb.). – ISBN 0–335–09788–X (pbk.)
    1. Organizational change.   2. Corporate culture.   I. Title.
II. Series.
    HD58.7.A48   1993
    658.4′06–dc20
                                                        93–25316
                                                            CIP

Typeset by Type Study, Scarborough
Printed in Great Britain by St Edmundsbury Press,
Bury St Edmunds, Suffolk

CONTENTS

ACKNOWLEDGEMENTS

My thanks are due to Graeme Salaman for his advice and wise guidance and to Pat Lee and her colleagues for their help and patience. Once again, I am grateful to Tom Keenoy and to Mike Reed for their benevolent interest and influence.

INTRODUCTION

A great deal of attention is being paid to organizational culture, to the ways in which it can be changed so as to bring about improved performance, greater concern with customer satisfaction and with quality. The extent to which cultural change is regarded as the necessary preliminary to the solution of hitherto intractable problems of the proper motivation of employees is reflected in the extent of the literature of excellence. Many large corporations in the private sector and an increasing number of public authorities are making determined efforts to bring about cultural renewal. In others, where there is less apparent concern with 're-culturization' even greater effort is being applied to change the normally accepted values shared by their inhabitants. The current debate about the alleged 'privatization' of the National Health Service (NHS), for example, can easily be seen as a more discreet attempt to substitute a culture of market responsiveness for one of professional control without an overt attempt to transform its culture. Much the same argument is taking place in universities, schools and the BBC.

If these are examples of the pursuit of cultural change, then they represent the choice of more covert means (changes in structure, personnel, financial control and funding which are intended to produce a new culture) than the strategy

1

recommended in the literature of cultural management. In the latter the rhetoric of cultural change often comes first, new values and beliefs precede new behaviour and new structures: first change the culture and all else is believed to follow.

The difference between the covert and the overt, between structure and rhetoric, is significant and it illustrates one of the difficulties we face in the discussion of cultural management: unless care is taken, there will be no end to it.

Change, accidental or intended, is a commonplace of managed organizations. We are concerned here with the deliberate attempt to bring about change in the culture of organizations by their managements; with managing culture. The trouble is that culture is an abstract and general concept and it can be influenced by changes that have nothing to do with culture: culture both influences systems and behaviour and is influenced by them. So, a book about the management of culture could easily turn into a book about the management of everything; production systems, pay structures, markets and the rest, because they are all likely to influence culture. The first arbitrary decision in a necessary process of exclusion is that we are not concerned with influences upon culture that are beyond the influence of managers. Thus, racial, national, regional and religious influences upon culture have nothing to do with this particular case, although such wider considerations obviously affect organizations and set limits to how far their cultures can be changed. We must also distinguish between those influences which, although well within the scope and power of management to influence culture, do not operate directly upon the cultural scene. A change in the design and layout of an office or a production control system, even though it may be intended to bring about a change in culture will be treated here as essentially different from the attempt to change culture by cultural means. 'Managing culture', for our purpose, means the management of cultural characteristics rather than the management of the structural environment even when it is intended to bring about cultural change by indirect means. To take the earlier example, changing the funding of the NHS is not our business here even though – if it is successful – it will change the culture of the service, but the acquisition of a new 'philosophy' by Shell or British Petroleum (BP) or British Airways (BA) is our concern, a

2

part of the management of culture. This is not meant to be a pedantic distinction. It is necessary to provide some sort of boundary for a subject that is notoriously loose but it should not be taken to imply that these more formal changes are unimportant. On the contrary, the argument to be presented will suggest that the attempt to manage culture without structural change is likely to be at best ineffective and at worst dangerous, that structure is not only a necessary accompaniment of cultural change but that it often provides the best means of achieving it.

There is another source of confusion that it will be impossible to avoid. All settled and identifiable communities, nations, ethnic groups and organizations, possess cultural characteristics as signifiers of their identity: their members tend to share systems of values and beliefs and to transmit them to newcomers by established means. In the case of business and administrative institutions, these characteristics are what we call 'organizational cultures'. But organizations are also prone to take a particular view of themselves, for purposes of advertising or public relations or, sometimes, to motivate their employees to greater loyalty and effort. This inspirational view of what the culture of the organization is may differ from the way it seems to its inhabitants or to an observer. It may not even be meant to be accurate because it is intended to influence rather than describe; accuracy may be the last requirement if the intention is to change the frame of people's perceptions of reality.

This more self-conscious view of an organization's culture needs to be distinguished from the system of values and beliefs that are implied rather than explicit, the values in action, that are revealed in the behaviour, policies and practices of its inhabitants and its history. The distinction is between the espoused version of culture and the real, between the proposed and the descriptive, between what should be and what is. In order to retain the distinction we shall call the former 'corporate culture' and the latter 'organizational culture'. For the most part we shall be concerned with corporate culture – although the two may be difficult to separate in practice, for reasons that we shall discuss – because it is the self-conscious and the espoused that is represented in most attempts to manage culture. Indeed, the management of culture implies some determination on the part of its managers to depart from the culture that exists, to change it because of some perceived inadequacy. It is in the difference between the two and the method of moving from the one to the other that much of the interest and significance in the current concern with the management of culture lies.

The extent of that concern is considerable. The pursuit of cultural change is deemed to be synonymous with the pursuit of excellence and therefore of unquestioned utility. The very wide claims made for the success of cultural change have led to a state of high excitement in which it has been hailed as one of the most significant advances in the history of organizational studies and as the herald of a new renaissance in management.

If these claims are correct, the matter is obviously worth attention and an attempt to understand what is going on. This attempt will begin with a brief account of some descriptions of cases of organized cultural change and an assessment of their success. Next, we will look at the goals pursued in these processes of change and at the reasons for the selection of organizational culture as a means to achieve them. Then we shall turn to the methods employed for bringing about change and the ingredients that are apparently associated with success, although it must be stressed – less false expectations are aroused – that this book does not set out to tell anyone 'how to do it'.

All this is a necessary preliminary to the real purpose of the book, which is to raise some critical questions about the claims made for cultural change and to reveal some confusions that have arisen in advancing them. The issues raised will include:

1 The meanings given to culture and the uncertainties and contradictions that are likely to follow hidden ambiguities and misunderstandings as to its depth and complexity.
2 The intensely practical question as to whether the real intention is to change culture and values or whether, for the most part, change in the behaviour of people is sufficient for the organization's purpose.
3 The consequences of change in culture and whether, in such a rich and diverse field, they can ever be accurately predicted to follow from the change programme that was intended to bring them about.

4 The peculiar dangers that attend the attempt to change 'meaning' in organizations that are likely to remain bureaucratic and directive and, therefore, easily convinced that subordinate compliance is evidence of inner conviction.

Finally, we shall try to look at the realities of organizational culture and its ingredients of morality, tradition and negotiated order so that we can suggest that a better understanding of culture is likely to improve the performance and practice of managers. The belief, on the other hand, that culture represents an Aladdin's lamp that will provide its owner with every wish will be questioned both as to its truth and its threat to the owner's grasp of reality. Cultural change is a slow process, it can be assisted rather than controlled but, in given circumstances, its pursuit might be worth while as long as it is not sought as a facile, cosmetic and transitory change.

NEW CULTURES AND HOW TO GROW THEM

There are innumerable snapshots and pen portraits of cultural change brought about by corporate leaders, but longitudinal accounts are rare. Pettigrew's (1985) study of change over a period of some twenty years in ICI was supported by close observation and access both to directors and to documentation. It shows that the attempt to change corporate culture was accompanied by complex political processes and structural adjustment. A more limited attempt to bring about a relatively sudden transformation in corporate culture was Shell UK's introduction of a new 'philosophy of management'. As it happens, two quite independent accounts have been presented of two successive attempts to introduce change in Shell, the first in the 1960s, the second in the 1980s. The account of the first attempt is taken from Blackler and Brown (1980).

The case of Shell UK

In 1965, a study group of Shell UK Refining Ltd suggested that a new philosophy of management should be prepared and the services of the Tavistock Institute of Human Relations were engaged to help to write it. The reasons given for this departure included the need to seek an organizational response to rapid technological change in circumstances of accelerating uncertainty and complexity and the belief that an organization could retain cohesion and the ability to respond appropriately if the majority of its members could subscribe to a common set of values. This need was emphasized by the perceived problem of motivating employees to work effectively, heightened by the failure of the traditional apparatus of management controls. The problems could be met, it seemed, only by the formulation and promulgation of a statement of management philosophy. The ingredients of the analysis–technological change, turbulence, the inadequacy of bureaucratic controls – and of the proposed solution – motivation through commitment to common values – are remarkably similar to the current concern with the management of culture.

The methods to be employed were also similar to those familiar in contemporary programmes of cultural management. First, the cascade: the attitudes of senior managers were to be changed, those, in turn, would change the attitudes of subordinate managers and finally, in due time, the attitudes of the shop floor would fall into line. Because employees were to be internally motivated – the external coercion of bureaucracy had, after all, been rejected as inappropriate – there had to be open participation in the programme, but within the constraints set by the principles of the philosophy.

In October 1965, the Employee Relations Planning Unit and the Tavistock advisers (joint authors of the philosophy statement) discussed the statement at a three-day conference with top management and agreed a programme of further dissemination to senior staff. A series of two and a half day residential conferences for senior staff members followed, each chaired by a senior refinery manager. During some of the conferences, amendments to the philosophy statement had been suggested but top management decided during the course of the conferences that modifications should not be made. Successive waves of meetings and discussion lapped over all parts of the organization until departmental members, foremen, trade union officials and shop stewards had all been introduced to the new philosophy.

7

The introduction of the new philosophy was described as a success both by members of management and in the external academic community. The published accounts, in 1971, 1972 and 1975 'offered largely uncritical descriptions of what took place' (Blackler and Brown, 1980: 119). Within the company, the success of the new philosophy seemed to be epitomized in the changes at the wax plant at Stanlow, seen by some as 'the biggest experiment of the whole philosophy exercise'. But, the authors add, 'for many people the discovery that outside Shell these changes were presented as highly successful just at the time when things appeared to be going badly wrong led to a disillusionment with both the philosophy in particular and with applied social science in general' (Blackler and Brown, 1980: 89). The authors' own considered verdict was that the intention to change the philosophy of Shell management failed, that the change strategy was ill conceived and badly executed and that it led 'to a betrayal of people's expectations' (p. 120) and that, at Shell Haven and at Stanlow, 'there is very little tangible evidence . . . of any broad cultural change' having been achieved (p. 127). The responsibility for this failure, in the authors' judgement, lay with an aspect of social science theory rather than with management for taking its advice. This is the fashionable cult of 'organization design', 'largely concerned with the creation of conditions to help people communicate more openly together in a spirit of truth and cooperation. Such is evidently a commendable thing to do, but (as the Shell project so vividly illustrated) it is also open to abuse if conducted in disregard of the reality of competing interests and differential power bases in business organizations' (p. 161). It is not the managers so much as the brand of social scientists they consult who are prone to a dangerously unrealistic and naive view of social relationships in organizations.

Shell continued

That is not the end of the Shell story, however. In the 1980s, once again the company found itself faced with a turbulent business environment, volatile markets, intense competition and, a new factor, over capacity. Once again the company faced the necessity of achieving the management of change, improved structure and operational efficiency. And, once again, the key to success was identified as improved communication with employees. The failure of the new philosophy was apparently forgotten:

> a key factor emphasised in this process of self-analysis and improvement was the support and cooperation of employees. In the generation of this support and cooperation communication as the basis of employee involvement was stressed. A central theme of the company's employee relations policy was communication, with an ongoing 'Cascade' exercise to inform the workforce about the business environment and the rationale behind company strategy. (Starkey and McKinlay, 1988: 89)

The survival plan for the Carrington Chemical plant depended on the abolition of job demarcations, the reduction of organizational layers from six to four, the removal of the shift foreman grade. Leaner organization, flexible work arrangements and the reduction of supervision all imply the necessity for greater cooperation between workers and the increased exercise of responsibility. Once again, it would seem, the company arrives at the conclusion that values must change in order to improve motivation and, once again, the same sort of means to the end are chosen: 'the leadership supplies the vision and impetus to change. The problem is then one of translating this strategic vision into widespread action. Here organization development (OD) consultants – internal and external – play a key role' (Starkey and McKinlay, 1988: 99). 'Vision' comes from the leadership – one or two senior company managers – the OD consultants then contribute 'specific skills . . . used to generate ways of helping in the implementation of the change process', team building, 'getting the management thinking right for handling the changes' (p. 100).

The account of these more recent changes at Shell acknowledges that the new philosophy and its failure is remembered with some anxiety: 'it was almost a dirty word'. This time it would be different. The difference between the old and the new programmes of change seem to amount to a different orientation on the part of OD, that it was no longer 'nice, soft, cuddly', that it was not to be seen as an end in itself – it surely never was, as Blackler and Brown observed, it had 'a clearly instrumental orientation regarding other people's attitudes and values' (Blackler and Brown, 1980: 22) – but that it was now strategically related to business objectives. However, just in case the difference remains obscure, they have changed the label: 'our senior OD consultant refuses almost to talk about OD anymore and much prefers organizational effectiveness as a title. OD still has that baggage from way back' (Starkey and McKinlay, 1988: 101).

Starkey and McKinlay give an account, as was their purpose, of change strategy and innovation in work practices in four companies. In the case of Shell, they provide little by way of evaluation of the changes they describe. They do say that there are similarities between the new philosophy programme of the 1960s and the programme of the 1980s. The emphasis continues to lie on cooperative employee relations, on consensus management, 'there are distinct continuities with the principles underpinning the New Philosophy of the 1960s, particularly in the emphasis on involving employees in the process of change' (p. 104). Their description suggests several similarities: in the circumstances and responses to them that initiated the interventions, in the intended consequences and the methods they were meant to achieve and in the underlying conviction that values had to change, a new philosophy had to be accepted, a new culture had to be introduced. If this is the case two questions arise; why was an acknowledged failure replicated, and will the replication be any more likely to work than its predecessor?

The first of these questions must be postponed for the moment because it raises some issues that we shall come to later and that occupy an important part of our argument about the motivation for cultural change.

The second question cannot be reliably answered because we do not have the careful, scholarly and balanced consideration available to us that was provided by Blackler and Brown (1980) in their examination of the new philosophy. The indicators, however, do not seem to be positive. The very similarities suggest that little had been learned and that the programme leaders were driven to their convictions by something other than a concern for evidence of reliability in the strategies they chose. In the first instance, Blackler and Brown reported that the redundancy programme of 1964 left a legacy of mistrust towards the company, that the tradition of loyalty had been demolished. The second programme was also accompanied by redundancy. At Shell Haven, manning levels were halved between 1981 and 1984, head office staff were reduced by 28 per cent, the survival of the Carrington plant required the work force to be halved. Indeed one of the explanations offered of a difference between the two approaches is that the second is more realistic, tougher, a mixture of the open and informative and the hard and assertive (Starkey and McKinlay, 1988: 103). There is little doubt that the accompaniment of the disturbance of redundancy to programmes of cultural change intended to internalize new values makes it difficult to determine whether change has been accepted or whether it appears to be so as the result of understandable expediency. Finally, the opinion of a senior Shell executive suggests a weary acknowledgement that there is little new about change programmes: 'we all thought it was the new millenium, but, as I say, we've been round the course two or three times since' (p. 106).

Whether it worked or not – a question that may well be determined in these complex organizational settings by quite extraneous circumstances, unplanned interventions and unforeseen consequences – is not as significant as the criticisms made by Blackler and Brown of the insecure foundation of social science theory upon which these consultant driven strategies are based. If they are right then all such adventures are as likely to fail as they are to succeed.

The case of British Airways

The transformation of British Airways from a moribund loss maker to the highly profitable 'world's favourite airline' in ten years represents an impressive management achievement. It is also claimed as a notable success for the planned management of corporate culture (Hopfl, 1993).

In the merging of the British Overseas Airways Corporation and British European Airways in 1974, British Airways had created an organization in which centralized bureaucracy was reinforced by something of the arrogance of the old Imperial Airways. British Airways was a service organization characterized by the emblems of uniform and rank, its ethos represented by its aircrew. Its apparent lack of concern for customer satisfaction was reflected in its substantial financial losses, estimated in 1981 to be running into £250 million in two years. A reduction in staff of 9,000, the shedding of routes and the sale of aircraft helped to produce an operating surplus of £180 million in 1982–3. Lord King (then Sir John) had been appointed chairman in 1981, to be followed in 1983 by Sir Colin Marshall as chief executive.

Marshall identified the ingredients of continuing success as a necessary determination to improve customer service and the motivation of managers and staff to achieve this end as a first priority. Consultants were appointed, research into customer attitudes and requirements carried out, surveys conducted of employee opinions and concerns and the reduction in the training budget reversed. The first of many drives, 'Putting People First' was launched in 1983. These initiatives were paralleled by organizational changes producing a new slimmer and flatter organization structure in which five sections reported directly to Marshall, the reduction in the number and function of committees and the 'retirement' of seventy senior managers. A third ingredient in a massive attempt to change the behaviour and the outlook of BA was the creation of a much more visible and dynamic leadership.

Leadership is frequently said to be associated with change in corporate culture and much of its influence is believed to depend on the successful leader's charismatic character. Sir Colin Marshall was credited with much of the success of the turnround in BA's culture. He took every opportunity to communicate the new message of personal responsibility for customer concern and for getting details right. He met and talked to employees, recruits, managers, passengers and, if things were not done properly, he did them himself. Yet he has been described as possessing rather a remote personality. Legendary stories accumulated about his achievements and style. Just like the stories of great military leaders, he was credited with turning disasters into victories by his personal example in the face of the enemy.

On the first day of the introduction of the new Super Shuttle service a log jam of customers at the BA desks threatened breakdown. When all seemed lost and with no one capable of help, 'I happened to see out of the corner of my eye that one of the managers was helping. Guess who it was – Marshall.' All was well. That story was told by Michael Levin, the American consultant brought in by Marshall. Levin certainly seems to have possessed, if not the necessary charisma for achieving cultural change, then the conspiratorial qualities for its stage management. Levin has been described as 'an ex-Green Beret, ex-CIA operative and a self-proclaimed expert in 'psychological warfare' (*The Independent on Sunday*, Business, 14 February 1993).

Sir Colin, with the approval of Lord King, certainly proceeded with real interventions calculated to change the way BA did things. Research programmes were set up to reveal the attitudes and expectations of customers and of staff and they demonstrated a dangerous gap between what was being delivered and what was needed. As a result, the earlier cut-back in staff training was reversed and the first of many well publicized campaigns, 'Putting People First', was launched in November 1983. The intention was to put 12,000 staff involved in customer contact through a two-day course of training in personal attitudes, each rewarded by a personal visit from Sir Colin. The programme generated a demand that other managers should be regarded as suitable for treatment and a series of courses, Managing People First, was set up for 1,400 managers. A third programme, 'A Day in the Life', in 1985, was directed at improving inter-functional cooperation and removing departmental barriers to its achievement.

Once again, these extensive training programmes were not conducted in isolation from other real and very visible initiatives aimed at changing the structure, systems and behaviour of BA's personnel. The most significant of these must be the privatization of BA in 1987, following the opening of Terminal 4 in 1986 and confirming the consistency of the change to a market based, customer driven definition of service. Performance related pay systems were introduced based on performance appraisal. The competitive, even predatory attitude of BA to competitors was demonstrated by the take over of British Caledonian in 1988 –

itself an illustration of the effects of two distinct corporate cultures being joined, but not necessarily mixed. In BA customer teams were set up to promote better quality service. A mission statement eventually emerged followed by objectives, the most memorable of both being the resolve 'to be the best and most successful airline in the world'. Throughout the continuing programme of planned change, rhetoric was accompanied by real and concrete change, not only in structures and systems but in equipment and machinery so that the drive for better service was not impeded or turned sour by material breakdown.

It worked. BA became profitable and won awards confirming its view of itself as the finest airline in the world. But, just as it is impossible in the complexities of organizational change, to attribute cause to a specific agency – particularly to one that is itself as complex as culture – we can be no more certain that the management of culture in BA was responsible for success as it was for subsequent embarrassment.

In March 1992, Richard Branson sued Lord King for libel in the course of BA's response to the former's repeated allegations of unfair and illegal competition by BA against his Virgin Atlantic airline. After lengthy investigation and denial, BA apologized in Court on 11 January 1993, agreeing to prevent such activities continuing and to pay substantial costs. Subsequently, there was much talk of olive branches and of new and less confrontational relationships. BA denied that the 'dirty tricks' had been sanctioned by its Board. Mr Branson threatens to take legal action in the USA for £30–£40 million in compensation for the damage claimed to have been done to his business. Meanwhile, 'fresh evidence has emerged that British Airways employees have continued a "dirty tricks" campaign against Virgin Atlantic to woo away its customers' (*The Independent*, 23 February 1993).

It is just as unreliable to attribute these sorry events to the management of BA's corporate culture as it is to credit cultural management with the company's success but if the claim to success is impressive so must be the criticism: 'typically staff do not behave shabbily unless the corporate culture encourages them' (John Gay, *Sunday Telegraph*, City and Business, 17 January 1993).

A provisional judgement

The case for cultural change as a sufficient prelude to business success has, on the basis of Shell and BA, not been made. In the first case it fails because the misapplication of social science was not reinforced by structural support. In the second, it fails because there was sufficiently extensive structural change to make it impossible to determine how far culture was responsible for improvement. From this paradox it might be reasonable to conclude that the case for culture cannot win: if change is confined to culture it will not work, if accompanied by structural change it cannot be isolated as crucial to success.

But there is no shortage of reports of startling success, of corporate cultures transformed with invigorating results for their companies' performance. Accounts of corporate success attributed to the beneficent effect of cultural change are widely available in Peters and Waterman (1982), Deal and Kennedy (1982), Kanter (1985) and others. Many of these accounts are brief, anecdotal stories of the dramatic impact of founders, leaders, heroes, in establishing or rescuing their enterprises. Deal and Kennedy begin by pointing to a coincidence that they had noticed in a survey of companies 'known to' McKinseys; eighteen of some eighty companies surveyed possessed qualitative beliefs or values and all the eighteen were outstanding performers. Peters and Waterman start from much the same position, an elucidation of 'the lessons to be learnt from America's best-run companies'. The lessons stem from the claimed association between success and the possession of strong cultures. The conclusion from much of the cultural literature is that the possession or the creation of a strong culture will lead to economic success. That is as may be, but the case for the management – the deliberate change – of corporate culture in order to bring about success is a different one, going beyond the claimed (but contested) association between strong cultures and business success.

In their examination of Shell's new philosophy experience, Blackler and Brown (1980) severely criticized the reliability of that branch of social science which it depended upon. Whether or not the case for cultural management is founded upon unsound logic or flawed theory will not stop it in its tracks. There remains the claim that cultural management is supported by empirical evidence of an impressive association between companies with similar cultural characteristics and those demonstrating business success. Such claims are the subject of the narratives briefly set out in the well-known texts. Those, too, have been challenged, the subsequent business performance of the 'excellent' companies named by Peters and Waterman (1982) was no better than the performance of other companies selected at random. The explanation of those that were singularly successful lay in quite different areas, such as size and growth strategy (Hitt and Ireland, 1987). More generally, the assertion that organizational cultures can be managed at all, let alone that the change can favourably influence business performance, has been questioned (Schein, 1985: xii; Smith and Peterson, 1988: 121).

If logic, theory and evidence combine to induce scepticism about the claims made for cultural management, why does the case continue to attract wide attention?

David Guest (1992) outlines an answer to the question which acknowledges the sense of the 'excellence' case in countering the rational-analytic model of management with important reminders of the importance of informal and qualitative aspects of good management. Its popularity rests upon its simplicity, its timeliness, its winning concern with success and, by implication at least, its marketing promotion of McKinseys (pp. 12–18). The explanation for the excitement generated by cultural management further rests on the growing concern with the economic plight of the West coupled with the comforting belief that we can do something about it quickly and painlessly, simply by changing our values.

2

GOALS AND ASPIRATIONS

The current interest in the management of culture and in the creation of corporate cultures can be explained in terms of two related processes, the first historical, the second transformational.

The first goes back to the earliest misgivings about the efficacy of the development of scientific and administrative management in which there were three elements; F. W. Taylor's (1911) attention to job analysis and design, Fayol's concern with organizational structure, and Ford's articulation of production planning to market control. If the generic term 'scientific management' is applied to these three developments it has produced incalculable improvements in efficiency and material well-being. A convenient point for identifying a reaction against it is frequently identified with the Hawthorn experiments at Western Electric, 1927–32 – there were, in fact, earlier criticisms, but they were based on social and moral grounds and so do not count in the context of a common concern with efficiency. The managerial reaction against the first great managerial movement was grounded in the contention that it did not work. It rested on the argument that, in many circumstances, a rational and mechanistic analysis of the control of labour was to be based upon a clear distinction between thought and execution; even the routine shovelling of pig iron by the famous Schmidt was to be closely prescribed by management's prior determination of the most scientific methods of shovelling. Hawthorn uncovered evidence of defensive control exercised by members of working groups sufficiently powerful to undermine and overturn the rational expectations of managers for their performance. Working, 'primary', groups set their own standards and had access to unofficial means for their enforcement. They also had their own leaders.

These alarming revelations followed two or three decades in which social scientists had established that their knowledge of psychology could be employed to improve selection processes and reduce training time and training costs, at least at the level of manual operations. The progressive recruitment of the social scientists to solve practical management problems was described by Loren Baritz in *The Servants of Power* (1965). Hawthorn marked the extension of this recruitment to new servants, social psychologists and sociologists. A further extension of the interest created by Hawthorn – sometimes labelled neo-human relations – came with a reinterpretation of the Marxist concept of alienation in a politically neutral context. Against the theoretical background of Lewin (1951) and of Maslow (1943), it was argued that human beings had potential for cooperation in work that stemmed from their needs, once their basic material and survival requirements were met, for self-expression and self-actualization.

Writers like Likert (1961) and Douglas McGregor (1960) emphasized the counter-productive nature of a rational systems approach to organization in which subordinate employees played their unthinking part in the mechanistic ordering of tasks ordained by managers who were themselves ordered into place in prescribed administrative structures. More open, involving, participative, job designs would enable employees to achieve their own personal goals while at the same time attaining the goals of the organization. The gap between organizational plans and human delivery would be closed by the construction of more humane organizations. 'Theory X' was held to exemplify rigid, mechanistic organizations and the belief that work was alien and would be performed only with reluctance in return for reward and in fear of punishment. 'Theory Y' represented the realization that work could be a reward in itself, fulfilling natural aspirations that could be met by job design and organization that took account of human potential. There was an odd symmetry in the way that the new application of social science reflected Taylor's physical scientific management – which acknowledged that restrictive effort on the part of the worker was a rational reaction on his part to inefficient management – by recognizing that alienation followed repressive management: social scientific management had followed scientific management, each promising better productivity. Argyris (1964) sought to demonstrate that psychological withdrawal, resulting in industrial pathologies like absence, labour turnover and industrial disputes, was the inevitable result of organizations designed to exclude human capacities for cooperation and self-expression. With the extension of the recommendation for change from the design of the task to the design of the organization itself, organization design or OD marked the latest application of social science to repair what came to be seen as the crippling deficiences of scientific management and rational systems.

In this way a tradition of 'soft' management theory and advice came to oppose the 'hard' theory that had preceded it. An unnecessary and continuing relationship of hostility continues to exist between them. Administrative science and Taylorite job design was intended, and continues, to contribute control and coordination in work. Both qualities still exist and there is no evidence of their imminent disappearance from employment. Indeed, much of the formation of organizational culture is attributed to the influence of structures created by that movement.

That influence is now deemed to be inappropriate. To the criticism of the sterility of rational systems in failing to liberate the productive capacity of individuals and groups is now added the charge that the well-ordered, compartmentalized hierarchies of bureaucracy are unfitted to the contemporary world of global competition, rapid technological development and turbulent market conditions. Control had been made conditional upon predictability, but if nothing could be predicted any longer, control seemed irrelevant. 'The era of strategic planning (control) may be over; we are entering the era of tactical planning (response)' (Kanter, 1985: 41). Bureaucracy had its time and place, 'ideally suited to the era of mass production' (Sadler, 1988: 125) but now 'there is a growing international consensus that for the Western countries economic renaissance is dependent upon the cultural transformation of large-scale business, and in particular on the extent to which decaying bureaucracies can be replaced with dynamic organic cultures' (p. 127). Deal and Kennedy 'see a revolution on the horizon . . . a breakdown of the large, traditional hierarchical organizations that have dominated in the past . . . We see it as a no-boss business. We call it the *atomized* organization. For it to work, strong cultural ties and a new kind of symbolic management will be required' (Deal and Kennedy, 1982: 127).

Both these statements suggest that the old bureaucracies have to be replaced by cultures. This is because, if the apparatus of formal control is to be dismantled, there must be some means of assuring that the organization, albeit atomized, remains an organization, at least to the extent that it is sufficiently goal directed to survive. If no one can be controlled because turbulence and technology combine to make them uncontrollable, if responsibility is to be pushed downwards in a drive for flexibility and if there can be no central direction because there is no centre and no directorate, some safeguard must be found against potential anarchy. The result of everyone becoming entirely entrepreneurial might be overly exciting; the shareholders, at least, might be disturbed.

The answer to the problem is found in 'directed autonomy': employees *must* be trusted and they *can* be trusted because they will be brought to share the same values and meanings, the same culture. They will then be able safely to exercise autonomous judgement because their dismantled organization will know that that judgement will be exercised in its own continuing interest. Culture is not only a necessary substitute for bureaucracy, it will be more effective because, borrowing from the OD wing of the soft school, we know that bureaucratic control never worked well anyway. It may be noticed in passing that a shift has taken place away from OD in the new organizational thinking. The OD tradition, represented in Shell's new philosophy by Tavistock consultants, argued from a set of beliefs about human capacity and motivation, to be released by organizational re-design to mutual benefit. The new, cultural reconstruction movement, argues from the urgent requirements of the market and technology that change has to take place and that culture must accommodate it. It is this shift that underlies the claim, reported by Starkey and McKinlay, that Shell's second attempt at change in the 1980s is different, more hard nosed than the old OD driven new philosophy.

The application of anthropology

The market driven necessity for cultural reconstruction is accompanied and reinforced by a continuation of the search for help from social science. We left that story with the recruitment of the social psychologists and sociologists – contributers to the development of OD – in the construction of open, participative organizations. The next step in that development was to be the recruitment of the last of the social scientists, the anthropologists.

Until then, anthropology seemed to be the most respectable and the least serviceable of the social sciences, singularly removed from the interest of managers. From its early preoccupation with the customs and culture of remote Pacific islands, studied because of their isolation from outside influence, anthropology had moved to urban societies, street gangs, occupational communities and the work place. The intention was detached from any concern with utility and the ideal was scientific objectivity. It is difficult to specify the point at which this academic activity came to be seen as providing practical assistance to managers. Morgan (1986: 111) suggests that it might have been occasioned by the OPEC oil crisis of 1973. Turner's study (1971) of the industrial sub-culture was intended to improve the understanding of cultural influences in work, but that educative aspiration, valuable though it is, could not and did not create 'the greatest anticipation, excitement and debate' within the field of organizational behaviour, providing 'a topic with few "ifs and buts", which is readily comprehended, and which can be applied immediately' (Wilson and Rosenfeld, 1990: 234). Culture, the

21

scholarly concern of the anthropologist, has become 'one of the key concepts from organizational behaviour to be translated so readily into the world of the practising manager' (p. 234).

Something has suffered in the translation. Wilson and Rosenfeld distinguish an analytic from the applicable cultural school. We might label the anthropologist's concern with culture as descriptive: what all the excitement is about is prescriptive, the concern of the consultant that culture should be changed rather than understood. Early studies of communities showed that they maintained themselves through economic relationships but that they were also sustained by patterns of belief, values and meaning transmitted through traditions, symbols and stories. These cultural features influenced approved patterns of behaviour and proscribed others; what people did was strongly influenced by what they were taught to believe and to mean. The realization that behaviour is influenced by culture is the explanation for the excitement. The rest is all about the pursuit of excellence.

Argyris and the others communicated to OD consultants that mental health – psychological well-being, they called it – was a resource at the disposal of the organization and that, if it was wisely used, the organization would benefit from the wholehearted cooperation of employees that would be unlocked. It has been argued that the provision of mental health is a powerful instrument of control that aims more totally to enclose the subordinate in his or her organizational environment (Anthony, 1977). The extension to the concern with cultural management and control represents the latest, possibly the last, recruitment of the social sciences, the ambition to control meaning itself in the interest of the organization.

The potential rewards are great. They can best be described by moving, at this point, from the historical account with which we have been engaged, to what we called earlier the transformational explanation.

Transformation, from control to commitment

An alternative way of perceiving the historical development of the interest in organizational culture, is to see it as an attempt to

change the nature of the organization, to transform its fundamental character and the relationship between its members.
Etzioni (1961) analysed complex organizations according to the
kind of power they exercised over their lower participants, to the
kind of orientation of the subordinates – their involvement – and
to the congruence between the basis of power and orientation to
relationships of compliance. Power in organizations was coercive, based upon punishment; remunerative, based on reward;
or normative, on the allocation of symbolic rewards. The application of coercive power leads to alienative, negative or hostile
involvement of high intensity. Remunerative power illicits a
calculative involvement of low intensity which may be positive or
negative. Normative power is associated with moral involvement
of high intensity. Etzioni adds that 'most organizations tend to
emphasize only one means of power, relying less on the other
two . . . The major reason for power specialization seems to be
that when two kinds of power are employed at the same time,
over the same subject group, they tend to neutralize each other.'
Thus, 'the application of remunerative power makes appeal to
"idealistic" (pure normative) motives less fruitful' (p. 7). In the
same way, the manipulation of esteem and prestige symbols, 'an
important source of normative control', is not likely to be
successful in exercising control over industrial subordinates
(p. 36). This is a particular case of a general truth; cases of
congruent compliance in which involvement is appropriate to the
predominant kind of power are found more frequently because
congruence is more effective and organizations are under press-
ure to be effective. So, 'organizations tend to shift their compliance structure from incongruent to congruent types and
organizations which have congruent compliance structures tend
to resist factors pushing them toward incongruent compliance
structures' (p. 14).

If this were the case, why is it that industrial organizations,
centres of remunerative power and as such expected to pursue
calculative involvement as the most effective way to efficiency,
are to be found setting off in the opposite direction in a search for
something remarkably like normative power – the manipulation
of esteem and prestige symbols? Etzioni's analysis has stood the
test of time and is widely used to focus the essential difference in

power and authority between organizations staffed by professionals and enterprises concerned to control production workers, a difference in the nature of compliance. Is it the case that remunerative organizations are not behaving as they should or is the analysis wrong? More particularly, why are we bothering about a classification that seems to have nothing to do with the case, and that appears to be unable to address the concern with change in organizational culture?

One of several possible answers to this question is that there is an implicit assumption in Etzioni, not rare among sociologists, that there is a functionality about organizations that moves them in the direction of survival and, hence, efficiency. Organizations 'ought' to behave like this and, of course, there is always empirical evidence that they do, since the organizations cited and studied have survived. This is a version (there are several others) of the assumption of organizational rationality. If we question that assumption then we may see that the compliance framework actually succeeds in explaining what is going on while appearing to prove that it cannot happen.

Human resource strategy

Another method of changing corporate culture currently receiving attention is through human resource management (HRM): 'indeed, the achievement of HRM objectives requires the management of the organizational value system (culture) and this requires skilful implementation' (Ogbonna, 1992: 80). The concern of human resource management with cultural management is sometimes regarded as a defining characteristic, distinguishing it from personnel management. Discussing, somewhat sceptically, the extent of the difference, Legge says 'that most HRM models emphasize the management of the organization's culture as the central activity for senior management' (in Storey, 1989: 28). If there is little evidence that HRM serves as the generator of corporate culture, it is very likely to act as the messenger or change agent. Change in structure, performance appraisal, performance related pay, training programmes and counselling are all activities in which HRM is likely to be the repository of old skills available for new purposes; if it is the aim of the new chief executive to create a new culture, 'the policies necessary to achieve this are those of HRM' (Guest, 1990: 394).

The real importance of HRM in this process of cultural transmission, like much else about it, is questioned. Purcell (1989) finds it odd 'that the current wave of interest in human resource management is so optimistic and implies that a major reconsideration of personnel practice is under way. The belief is that corporate executives and line managers have discovered the need to encourage employee involvement, team work and integrated reward systems . . . as a crucial element of their corporate and business-unit strategies', odd because, although there are interesting experiments taking place, 'the material conditions for these to be translated into long-run strategic decisions placing human resource management at the, or even a, critical function in corporate strategy, do not exist. What ought to happen, as prescribed by the burgeoning literature, is a long way from being realized' (p. 90).

Guest agrees: 'even in the United States there are signs that the enthusiastic advocacy of HRM is being increasingly questioned' (1990: 394) and suggests that HRM can serve as a smokescreen for the pursuit of anti-unionism and reduction in the labour force. The need for smokescreens suggests that some uncomfortable contradiction between word and deed has to be concealed. The means of concealment may be to hand in the transformatory, synthesizing power of the cultural equipment that is available. While the enterprise is represented through its sensitive and thoughtful HRM policies, it can, with pride, reflect on its downsizing and 'manpower release' of 19,000 employees as the result of 'good cost control and our capital investment pro-gramme' (Keenoy and Anthony, 1992). Contradictions are not apparent and easily recognized because the culture of HRM is entailed by the culture of the market which defines excellence and cultural strength. Contradictions are obscured because the difference between reality and cultural construction is deliber-ately occluded; if the cultural construction succeeds in becoming our representation of our experience, it becomes our experience. HRM, says Guest, 'is encased in myths and legends. The legends are the case studies' like 'the use of quality circles at Lockheed.

They have turned into myth as their existence is cited to support quality circles long after they ceased to operate' (1990: 393).

But myths can move if they come to stand for our conception of reality. One of the problems about the cultural content of HRM is the suspicion that it represents someone else's conception of reality, held out of a special concern and a special interest: 'after all, it can be argued that HRM itself has a connotation of instrumentality, hence only the end result matters. If this is so, then HRM may have become the latest addition to the array of strategies that legitimate managements' attempts to tighten their control over the workers' (Ogbonna, 1992: 94).

It all turns on the distinction between what is and what ought to be, between the way things are and the way we – or someone else – would like them to be. Industrial organizations are, in Etzioni's terms, essentially remunerative and are held together by comparatively weak bonds of calculative compliance and involvement. Normative organizations, on the other hand, do not have to pay for compliance, indeed material reward is actually likely to be counter-productive, as well as expensive. The moral involvement of their members is comparatively strong, often evincing a commitment to shared goals, which they are capable of pursuing with zeal quite independently of the exhortations of their leaders. Confronted with the evidence of merely calculative involvement and, at some levels, even worse, actual alienation from the goals of the organization, it is hardly surprising that managers and their human resource strategists will wish for a transformation.

As it happens they are reinforced in this ambition by messages that convince them, coincidentally, it would seem, that the world is changing to an extent that professional, normative organizations are becoming the pattern. Coercive control was removed from serious consideration several decades ago by the social scientists' argument that it did, in fact, lead to alienation and inefficiency. New technology, new markets and new flexibilities now seem to demonstrate that the shared values and goals of professionals, along with their reliable judgement, must be incorporated into new organizations. Along with the historical search for higher levels of commitment, the normative organization is now presented as a choice that can be made – a practical alternative to the old, calculative, bureaucracies.

This is another way of seeing the attempt at transformation of organizational culture; as the substitution of commitment for systems of control that are now deemed to be expensive, ineffective and outmoded.

Before attempting to discover whether this transformation can be accomplished, whether culture can be purposefully changed, it is important to determine what it is that is to be changed, what is meant by culture.

3

DEFINITIONS

The question of definition has been avoided so far. It cannot be further postponed. If we are to determine whether organizational cultures can be managed and with what effect we must try to decide what we mean by culture.

Meek argues that the various theories fall into one of two groups (1992: 202–5). In one, culture is seen as something an organization possesses, 'Human relations theorists regard culture as something which an organisation has and which can be manipulated to serve the ends of management' (1992: 199); in the other, culture is embedded in the organization's history and structural relationships, 'culture is something an organisation is' (Smircich, 1985: 347). The former might be called the managerial view of culture, the latter the anthropological.

What cultures are

Cultures develop in communities which are distinctive from their neighbours and are held together by patterns of economic and social cooperation reinforced by custom, language, tradition, history, and networks of moral interdependence and reciprocity. As these are established and sedimented over time they lead to customary understandings and obligations, patterns of expectations that do not require to be calculated or defended. The ordinary transactions of life in a community depend upon implicit and unexamined assumptions and agreements about values and meanings. They depend, in other words, upon shared cultures. Communities and cultures are easily recognized in ethnic, national and regional entities but institutions may also possess the characteristics of communities with common cultures. They are layered within broader communities so that we begin to speak of sub-cultures. Thus Turner (1971) describes the features of the 'industrial sub-culture' which are identifiable within the wider culture of Western Europe or the United Kingdom. Within the world of industrial employment, marked similarities may become established in association with particular occupations or trades, 'occupational communities' like steelmaking or coal-mining in which the shared values and language of the particular industry mark its occupants as distinct from others. Members of professional groups can also exhibit a special way of looking at the world. Military institutions reinforce these differences by uniforms, traditions and language that is intended to be unintelligible to outsiders. Within these levels of sub-cultures – each necessarily sharing the understandings of the enclosing general culture – institutions of a more ephemeral nature may begin to develop cultural characteristics, if they persist in time and are capable of providing stable relationships for their inhabitants. So, within the industrial sub-culture or the occupational community, the particular firm can be recognized as possessing a distinctive and characteristic culture. ICI, Marks & Spencer, and Ford Motors are different from other firms in the same sector of industry or the same country. Their employees share the same national cultural characteristics – the firms could not otherwise survive in the broader community – but they are also differentiated by marked and recognizable sub-cultural features.

In most cases they did not acquire these distinctions as the result of deliberate effort or intention. They were often established in the first place by their founders, Alfred Mond, Henry Ford or, in the case of Marks & Spencer, the transforming activity and personality of inheritors like Sir Simon Marks or Lord Sieff.

Culture followed and grew out of the company's history, establishing a pattern of 'the way we do things here' which required a necessary conformity on the part of new recruits. Conformity was assured in the reasonably perspicacious newcomer by an informal process of induction and socialization no less effective because it lacked the ceremonial and symbolic features accompanying recruitment to a regiment of the line.

Distinctive organizational cultures grow and are established by similarities of required outlook and behaviour over time. That is why Smircich (1985) observes that organizations do not possess cultures, they *are* cultures, the cultural characteristics and the organization are embedded in each other rather than existing as parallel but separate entities.

This quality of enmeshed coexistence paradoxically makes them peculiarly difficult to observe or classify, particularly by their inhabitants. What cultures are seems a natural part of the process of living, in no way remarkable to those who share them. They become more distinctive and recognizable, even odd, at the boundaries of organizations where the visitor becomes aware that there are words and meanings that are not easily understood. Smircich explains that cultural meanings are usually carried and displayed in symbolic form and can best be recognized in rituals, traditions and rites of passage.

This unconscious and unrevealed aspect of culture emerges in one of the most familiar definitions of organizational culture. Schein (1985) defines culture as:

> a pattern of basic assumptions invented, discovered or developed by a given group as it learns to cope with its problems of external adaptation and internal integration that has worked well enough to be considered valid, and to be taught to new members as the correct way to perceive, think, and feel in relation to those problems. (p. 6)

Schein adds that these basic assumptions, beliefs, values and meanings are 'shared unconsciously, in a taken for granted fashion' that makes them difficult to discern, even for those that hold them.

Cultures possess other characteristics that make them difficult to grasp. Turner (1971) points out that they are segmented both spatially and temporally; in the course of work, people walk out of one cultural enclosure and into another at different times of the day and periods of their lives, from a community to an occupational culture in which the rules, assumptions and values are different. Cultures change; indeed a persistent culture must demonstrate adaptive capabilities to significant changes in the environment and to newcomers who, although having to learn the cultural rules may also, particularly in the case of leaders, influence those rules. Cultures are thus both binding and integrative as far as their inhabitants are concerned, and open and adaptive to their surroundings. It may be their segmentation that helps to explain these dual and apparently contradictory features; they are not – apart from exceptional and significant examples – islands, their membership is diffuse, multi-cultural, mobile and communicative.

Culture and meaning

They also possess one potent ability that will go some way to explain recent managerial interest in their control; they are not only our constructions. They construct, to some extent, our view of what the world is; we make sense of it through the medium of our culture. Hampden-Turner (1990), after an account of success in cultural management and the means to achieve it, makes the significant point that cultures enable us to deal with contradictions in our experience of the events of life by a process of synthesis which incorporates the contradiction within our basic, taken for granted, assumptions: 'all corporate cultures take the form of mediated dilemmas' (p. 26). They may do even more than that, considerable though the feat is. Cultures may provide the basic, theoretical and perceptual building process upon which we rely to organize our inchoate experience. The means at their disposal to accomplish this epistemological understanding transcend the logical and the scientific. Narrative, story telling, is not bound by external consistency with the world because it imposes its own consistency upon it, organizing its random events into a coherent account for its listeners or readers (Ricoeur, 1984). And narrative is one of the many means by which cultures are formed and transmitted. The means include the rhetorical construction of communication, the persuasive use of language so as to influence the receiver's frame of reference, symbolism, metaphor and myth. 'Organizations exist as systems of meanings which are shared to various degrees. A sense of commonality, or taken for grantedness is necessary for continuing organized activity so that interaction can take place without constant interpretation and re-interpretation of meanings' (Smircich, 1985: 64). Such stabilities and constancies of meaning require to be distanced from the contradictions and confusions of reality and from the need to maintain stability and the need to change. Instruments are therefore needed that disguise such problems, 'metaphor simultaneously facilitates change and reinforces traditional values' (Pondy, 1983: 164). The mechanisms of cultural construction enable us to rely upon understandable and familiar meanings which are secure from the contradictions of everyday experience, meanings that can continue to be taken for granted. Hence, Pondy suggests that the significance of metaphor and myths 'is that they place explanation beyond doubt and argumentation' (p. 163).

The development of shared meanings in cultures is both a natural process of their evolution and a feature central to their identity: without them cultures do not exist and cannot survive. But to call their development 'evolutionary' begs several questions. The process is usually influenced, not to say controlled by the emergence and influence of important and powerful groups. The earth was once believed to be flat and the sun to revolve around it, not only because of the deficiencies of contemporary science but because of the cultural control exercised by the church – a distinction recognized by Galileo. It is not only in organizational cultures that we are aware of the significance of leaders in their formation. Cultures are, then, to some extent, deliberately shaped and maintained. Even when the process is not conscious and deliberate our meanings are constructed not only by what we are told but by our own experience and perception of our surroundings and those, for the most part, are not of our making. We inherit the world, we make sense of it and we are influenced in that sense by those who control it.

In other words, our meanings held in common are partly

handed down to us – the cultural baggage of tradition, reinforced by the material environment in which we live and which seems to reinforce our inherited beliefs – partly transmitted to us by powerful agencies, such as the law and education, and partly modified by our own critical or passive examination and experience.

The trap of cultural enclosure

In terms of the culture of work, its setting, organization and routines are likely to influence strongly our understandings and expectations. The primary features of technical and administrative arrangements, the hierarchies of control, the divisions of time and space and the rules of operation are largely unquestioned and so form some part of our expectations and understandings: if they were not largely shared, organized and cooperative work would be impossible. The influence of the rational and incontestable logic of work organization on our outlook or culture was extended by scientific management: 'the one best way' was not only a system of work control, it formed an element in cultural control (see Salaman and Thompson, 1980: chs 10 and 11). Culture is influenced by the way things are.

Influenced, but not determined. Lurking behind the complexities of culture are the ambiguities and confusions of ideology. Among the many definitions and explanations of the meaning of ideology is a distinction between its descriptive and its pejorative meaning (Geuss, 1981). An ideology in the descriptive sense 'will include such things as the beliefs the members of the group hold, the concepts they hold, the attitudes and psychological dispositions they exhibit' (p. 5). In the pejorative sense, ideology is seen as some kind of error, a basic misconception about the nature of reality, particularly of social reality. Thus it falsely takes some form of behaviour or some social phenomenon to be natural and outside control or it mistakes the interest of a minority to be the interest of the whole or more general society. Pejorative usages of the term often suggest that, in this sense, ideology implies delusion or false consciousness and, sometimes, that such delusion has been deliberately fostered or in some other way has come to represent a powerful group representing or believing its interest to be the general interest.

There is a good reason for confining our use of the word ideology to the pejorative: the alternative, descriptive meaning is extraordinarily difficult to distinguish from the meaning of culture. For this reason, in the context of this discussion, 'ideology' means a system of beliefs that have been deliberately inculcated by a group in its own interest, or that have come to be accepted by a group as unalterable when it is not. In this context, ideology is some form of misconception, deliberately fostered or accepted as the result of the experience of an environment falsely believed to be unalterable. In this usage – and it must be remembered that this is not the only usage – ideology is not the same as culture, but it can exercise a significant influence upon culture and, therefore, upon our view of reality. The 'ideological dimension', says Jameson, 'is intrinsically embedded within the reality, which secretes it as a necessary feature of its own structure. That dimension is profoundly *imaginary* in a real and positive sense; that is to say, it exists and is real in so far as it is an image . . .' (Jameson, 1991: 262).

So what can one say about the image, particularly when Jameson adds that it is 'its very unreality and unrealizability being what is real about it'? (p. 262). And what is there to say about ideology and the culture that it helps to form and maintain? It has been suggested, for example, that human resource management, as an agent of cultural transformation, 'is concerned with the management of beliefs, with the manufacture of acquiescence in corporate values, with the production of images' (du Gay and Salaman, 1990: 24). The attempt at cultural change rests upon ideological foundations, upon an ideological construction of the organization. As such, it is immune from a logical critique which reveals the contradictions between it and reality, 'for ideology does not "work" in a logical, intellectual fashion. It does not collapse as the result of a logical contradiction . . . ideology does not obey the logic of rational discourse' (Keenoy and Anthony, 1992). If such devices are intended 'to place explanation beyond doubt and argumentation', what more can be said about them. If ideology defines reality which is then encapsulated in a culture through which reality is perceived, then we are faced with a closed system into which it may be impossible to break. Certainly there would appear to be no way out by appealing to the empirical evidence, to the facts. There is, it would seem, nothing more to say.

The difficulty of saying anything, of submitting a culture to criticism, is related to its influence on meaning. If it is 'our' culture, it influences our meanings. This apparent impenetrability is, no doubt, one of the very great attractions in the prospect offered by cultural management.

Fortunately it remains possible to discuss culture, particularly organizational and corporate culture, in a critical fashion because certainly in the latter case – cultural formation has not yet taken place. The very evangelical zeal of the literature of corporate culture, the enthusiasm for 'excellence' and for a new renaissance in management values suggests that not all are yet of the faith and that there is still missionary work to be done. Indeed much of the point of this particular discussion is to challenge the faith of the missionaries and to suggest that, in some respects, their zeal is misplaced and possibly dangerous. If this were not the case, if corporate culture ruled the world or that part of it which we inhabit, the situation might be different; we might find it difficult to escape from a cultural enclosure, a consensus, in order to speak about it because its assumptions would be 'taken for granted'. But that is not so. If proof were demanded that we had succeeded in the claim to have broken out of culture's closed circle, it is provided by the questions that are being raised; its assumptions cannot be taken for granted because we have mentioned them. The emperor's clothes disappear only when we say we cannot see them.

A second difficulty in the protection of corporate culture from criticism is that even if its claims could not be resisted by reference to the facts, it might still be open to examination by reference to what we know, to what anthropologists have told us, about cultures and their features and functions. The question might be, not so much whether corporate cultures 'work' but whether they *are* cultures at all or simply misrepresentations. We shall return to this question later (in Chapter 8) in terms of the moral and community characteristics of cultures. At the present time we can at least ask what sort of corporate cultures are being proposed.

A third question in this period of formation concerns the likely consequences of the changes and methods under discussion and one question in particular, whether these proposals may strengthen or weaken the cultural bonds in organizations, increase or diminish the influence of leaders and contribute to organizational strength or weakness.

Finally, corporate culture makes itself vulnerable to criticism because it is bereft of the logical protections which attend ideology and culture. In the case of attempts to manage or to change corporate culture, the proposals for change enter the public arena of debate in a strange and most un-cultural way, demanding our explicit attention, asking us to pay substantial fees to hear the message or threatening us with unemployment if we refuse to listen. There is little that is stealthy. The new culture surfaces, comes clean and displays itself in a deliberate and self-advertised attempt to change or manage meanings and beliefs. In the circumstances, the least we can do is talk about it.

4

METHODS

If the culture of a community – ethnic, national, regional or occupational – is created by slow accretion, the culture of an organization may be more quickly acquired because it is more segmented and more partial in its enclosure of its members. Thus, while the creation of the culture of a community is never attributed to the influence of an individual, the culture of an organization is frequently explained by reference to one person. In circumstances in which the organization has been created by its founder who defined its boundaries, its purpose and its structure, it is likely that its cultural characteristics will owe much to his or her influence. There is a sufficient reason for not leaving it at that: the concern with changing or managing organizational culture means that the inheritance left by founders must be capable of modification, otherwise there could be no further discussion of the subject. And there is plenty of evidence that leaders, not necessarily founders, are important determinants of culture in organizations.

Leaders

If values are features of cultures, they are demonstrated and communicated in organizations by their leaders. Leadership is 'essentially to do with the creation of values which inspire, provide meaning for, and instil a sense of purpose to the members of an organization. The leader is the person who actively moulds the organization's image for both internal and external consumption and who suffuses it with a sense of direction' (Bryman, 1986: 185). Schein (1985), one of the most authoritative writers on the subject, believes that leaders and culture are as interdependent as to be two sides of the same coin and that it is possible that 'the only thing of real importance that leaders do is to create and manage culture and that the unique talent of leaders is their ability to work with culture' (p. 2). He accounts for their influence on culture in terms of five important influences: what they pay attention to; their reaction to critical incidents; their deliberate role-modelling and teaching, their choice of criteria for determining rewards and status; and by their criteria for recruitment, promotion, retirement or dismissal.

The question of who these leaders are, what qualities they possess and what relationships exist between them and their subordinates is a complex matter that cannot detain us here (see the discussion in Smith and Peterson, 1988, chs 7 and 8). Leaders, particularly of the inspirational kind, are often described as charismatic. Bryman (1986) reminds us that the current use of this term differs from the meaning given to it originally by Weber. We tend now to see it as a personal attribute residing in the leader; for Weber it was a quality recognized by others by virtue of which those possessing it are set apart and endowed with supernatural, superhuman or exceptional powers (p. 201, note 2).

Something like charisma is attributed to corporate leaders when they are called heroes. One of the chapters of Deal and Kennedy's (1982) *Corporate Cultures* is entitled 'Heroes: the corporate right stuff'. 'The hero is the great motivator, the magician, the person everyone will count on when things get tough' (p. 37). Since there is little purpose in addressing books or exhortations to a managerial audience which emphasize the importance of the inimitable and the extraordinary, the authors explain that 'heroes are symbolic figures whose deeds are out of the ordinary, but not too far out. They show – often dramatically – that the ideal of success lies within human capacity' (p. 37). What follows is in the tradition of Samuel Smiles' *Self Help* (1908), extraordinary tales of people who are not quite so extraordinary – the authors specifically inform us that heroism is not the same as charisma and does not require it – that they cannot be imitated by the rest of us or nurtured and developed by their organizations. They are not just managers, however. Deal and Kennedy tell the tale of Harold Geneen who transformed ITT 'into one of the fastest-growing and most profitable companies on the American business scene' (p. 42). Excellent, one might think. Subsequently, however, results went down, managerial blunders were revealed and there was even a whiff of financial scandal. And so it turns out that poor Geneen was no hero; he had been merely a manager all the time.

Congruence with the setting

Still, it cannot be contested that leaders, if they do not solely construct corporate cultures, have an important influence on their growth. Possessed of such power, in its various forms, it would be astonishing if they did not. But even Schein, for whom, as we have seen, culture and leadership are almost synonymous terms, explains that their influence upon culture needs support. Their influence can be contradictory and confusing: it is more likely to develop and support cultural construction if it is consistent with secondary features of the organization. These are:

- its design and structure
- the systems and procedures
- the lay-out of the physical environment
- narratives, myths and legends about the organization
- its formal expressions of policy and outlook.

Four of these features are material or systematic rather than ideational or cultural. Handy's (1985) well-known classification of cultures between power, role, task and personal, associates each with a particular form of structure (web, bureaucratic, matrix and cluster), but whether the culture influences the structure or follows it is a difficult matter to determine. Schein's secondary features suggests that congruent structural features will sustain the leader's cultural influence. A considerable and weighty opinion suggests the opposite, that the systematic planning of the work environment influences if not determines the values of its operators, including its managers.

Strategies

Four explanations of the strategy of cultural change emerge:

1 A process of normative change brought about by education and persuasion.
2 A process of coercion in which people with less power come first to do and then to believe what others with more power tell them.
3 A utilitarian process in which people follow their self-interest and are influenced by goals determined by their organizations and those who control them.
4 A conditioned process in which people's attitudes and values are virtually determined by their organizational environment which itself unconsciously reflects the prevailing values and expectations of society.

The first of these explanations of strategy influences the kind of intervention that Shell made in the promotion of its new philosophy: it characterizes the intentions of OD consultants and their conviction that new values can be introduced by education, training, communications, group participation and the like. But the belief in the power of rational persuasion is frequently supported by the more coercive influence of senior management and that, in turn, leads subordinates – including many managers who are not without their own coercive influence in the cascade of power as well as communication – to make perfectly rational, self-interested choices as to how they should behave. And all the time everyone is subject to the continuing influence of their organizational surroundings, to what Marx called the dull compulsion of economic activity or, to paraphrase the title of a well-known novel, the incredible heaviness of being.

All four influences are at work and may be inseparable in the accumulation of an organization's culture. But we are relieved, to some extent, of the irksome necessity of untangling them if we remember that we set out to examine the management of culture, the influence of managers and, in particular, their formulation of corporate culture. This is a reminder that before the instruments of change are discussed it is helpful to decide what is to be changed. There are at least three versions of the subject:

1 The anthropological view which sees organizational culture as organic and complex (Turner, 1971; Smircich, 1985), the function of which is analytical.
2 The consultancy view which posits some desirable state of culture which can be purposefully pursued and is instrumental to other ends: its function is prescriptive.
3 The corporate view which promulgates a unified and distinctive conception of culture, the function of which is to promote unity, prevent disaffection and influence public opinion.

The discussion in which we are engaged with 'managing culture' and, by implication, its change confines us to the second and third of these versions, with an occasional reminder of what the first has to tell us as a benchmark for comparison. The field is therefore usefully narrowed in terms of the methods by which change is to be pursued. It is confined to the methods that are available to managers and that are likely to be successful in the span of managers' active careers.

The methods that have been chosen by enterprises seeking to change corporate culture include programmes of education or training, sometimes available as packaged programmes, sometimes contributed 'in house' by the enterprise's own training specialists. They may be directed at particular areas of concern such as quality improvement or at general change in values consistent with the company's new philosophy or new vision of itself. The methods used may be directly concerned with explicitly teaching a vocabulary or a set of concepts which encapsulate understandings perceived to be appropriate or they may be more indirect and encompassing, intended to bring about a change in the employee's general outlook and values. The former will involve traditional methods of teaching, incorporating participative techniques. The latter may include group dynamics, transactional analysis, assertiveness training and leadership exercises.

Educational programmes are often associated with more straightforward communication programmes such as residential conferences or meetings from which the message is intended to 'cascade' down the levels of management so that each manager becomes responsible for changing the understanding and comprehension of the level below. More routine methods are employed in which news sheets, bulletins, audio- or video-tapes and posters are used. Other techniques include role modelling and role playing activities.

Education for public or private good is notoriously uncertain in its outcome and expensive in its input. A shorter way with the management of corporate values is to control access to membership of the organization, to conduct the recruitment and selection process so as to confine employment to those deemed acceptable in terms of their outlook and values. Thus one of the means by which organizations avoid adversarial relationships with employees and the recognition of trade unions is by screening out applicants for employment with radical backgrounds and combative personalities. The determination of culture by the control of those who have access to it is certainly influential; it would be absolute in its influence were it not for two difficulties; the uncertainty in specification of the type to be selected and the notorious weakness of selection methods, particularly in respect of personality.

A more sovereign remedy in the management of corporate culture is to control the membership of the organization by dismissing those employees who do not share its cultural requirements. This is much more certain a method than the selection process because the data on employees of long service is more reliable: in the language of the courts, 'anything known' can be taken into account before sentence is passed. The Xerox organization is reported to have pronounced, on its quality programme that: 'We clearly identify which executives are with us and which are not with us. We are patient with those that have to make the change but, in the end, if they do not adapt, they have to leave. Quite simply, if you do not want to be a quality performer, you do not work here' (Open University Unit B884, Block 3, p. 35).

42

Geoffrey Deith, ex-Managing Director of Toshiba Consumer Products said, in a video presented to job applicants by way of early warning, that he never wanted to hear the word 'absentee-ism'; 'we're trying to say right from the word go to anyone who may have a problem looking after a child with a cough or a cold at home, with no other parents in the area, that perhaps you should think again about coming to Toshiba Consumer Products. Because we won't have any spare people. It will be a lean and hungry company' (Williams et al., 1989).

All these are fairly direct methods of changing the values of an organization and its members by some form of cognitive appeal, by structural change, or change in personnel. Cognitive pro-grammes of reform are often overt, open and even when they are covert, when the objective of change is hidden from the audience and apparently unrelated to the educational content, it is easy to read the intentions of the educators. To that extent they are open to rational objection and debate, although the likelihood of that occurring may be reduced by the assistance of the utilitarian strategy so that employees understand that their acceptance of the educational programme coincides with their own immediate interest, whether they agree with it or not. Open programmes of change remain vulnerable to challenge, however, although they may provide the organization with the bonus of smoking out objectors so that they can be dealt with by other means.

If the comparative straightforwardness of the more direct methods of change is seen as a disadvantage, other means are available. The search for them provides one of the explanations for the current – and otherwise arcane – managerial interest in 'organizational symbolism'. Symbolism, as we have seen, is an important creator and carrier of culture. Symbols and narratives not only denote the existence of a culture, they can be and are used, by ecclesiastical, political and military institutions to reinforce and to create it. In the organization's search for effective corporate cultures, the manufacture and control of symbolism becomes a very practical activity.

A symbol is a sign which denotes something much greater than itself, and which calls for the association of certain conscious or unconscious ideas, in order for it to be endowed with its full meaning and significance . . . Symbols are signs which express much more than their intrinsic content; they are significations which embody and represent some wider pattern of meaning. (Pondy, 1983: 4–5)

Symbolism is not only 'carried' by organizational cultures; just as in other social institutions, it can be used and manufactured to create and sustain them.

Ideology

This reminds us of the ambiguity of the term 'ideology'; it can be used in the sense of a group of concepts that shape our perception of reality to the extent that reality is constructed by our conceptions of it. In what Geusz calls the 'pejorative sense', ideology means a misconception deliberately engendered by a powerful group defending by disguising its own special interests. Our understanding of the world of employment is moulded in both senses. We accept it because we are used to it, we have experienced no alternative, are by no means convinced that there can be an alternative; our practised engagement in it shapes our understanding and expectations. In this way we make our own sense of our industrial surroundings, but we are also offered help by the interpretations of our experience that are produced by the agencies of an industrial society and are communicated to us by interests that support its assumptions and practice and that are not predisposed to welcome change. Ideology in the first sense moulds understanding of our experience more or less innocently; in the second it is more deliberately deceptive; in both it is essentially conservative, grounded in the present. The means by which these supportive assumptions are transmitted are largely cultural, sometimes in the formal processes of socialization and education, sometimes by the more discreet processes of symbolic construction of meaning. Neither ideological construction nor cultural transmission are open processes to which rational analysis and criticism can be readily applied unless they are first uncovered, decoded and exposed by someone claiming to possess some expertise in the process – a structuralist critic, for example.

Both ideology and culture, in so far as they construct meaning, are available for the deliberate influence of meaning. The three strategies of change outlined on page 40 – educative, coercive and conditioned – all of them comparatively open to inspection, are followed by a fourth, the transmission of a prevailing ideology by the control of symbolic construction of meaning. It is in the nature of this process that both the result and the means of achieving it are concealed. The old OD strategies, the transforming behaviour of leaders and the missionary appeals of cascading communication and education are all the more visible when they are reinforced – incongruently, Etzioni would remind us – by rewards for their acceptance and punishments for rejection. But symbolic control of what we think the organization as being, what it *is* as far as our perception of it goes, is more secure from examination.

The influence of the market

Before we get to the shaping of the organization, our expectations for its behaviour, standards, values and of what it properly expects of us are largely determined by our understanding of its setting – the market. Once upon a time it was generally believed that the market was a place in which goods and services were exchanged at prices settled by many competing sellers bargaining with many buyers, all provided with adequate information. The market is no longer a place but a concept, it is the idea of the market that conditions policies both in the West and in an enthusiastic Eastern Europe. The idea of the market is sufficiently powerful to be immune from any concern with the contradictions of reality; that competitors strive for and reach domination, that competition is suppressed, pricing artificially sustained and demand created rather than satisfied. 'Reality' does not threaten the idea because the idea incorporates reality:

> the ideology of the market is unfortunately not some supplementary ideational or representational luxury or embellishment that can be removed from the economic problem and then sent over to some cultural or superstructural morgue, to be dissected by specialists over there. It is

somehow generated by the thing itself, as its objectively necessary afterimage'. (Jameson, 1991: 260)

the ideological dimension is intrinsically embedded within the reality, which secretes it as a necessary feature of its own structure. (p. 262)

The idea of the market is sovereign. The extent of its sovereignty at the high point of *laissez faire* is represented in Barry Unsworth's novel, *Sacred Hunger* (1992). The ship, *Liverpool Merchant*, well and specially built for the Atlantic slave trade, is beset by calms, storms and disease on her maiden voyage. Her experienced captain, Thurso, unprejudiced by personal interest except that 'he had his reputation to think of' and 'mindful of the need for lawful proceeding' conceives an idea:

Deaths among the negroes during the six days of bad weather had amounted to eighteen – ten men, five women and three boys. The ship had been considerably blown off course and a good number more were likely to die before Jamaica was reached. Those that survived would not look attractive to the planters that came to bid for them. Cargo dying aboard ship of so-called natural causes was quite worthless, whereas cargo cast overboard for good and sufficient reason could be classed as lawful jetsam and thirty per cent of the market value could be claimed from the insurers. (p. 382)

Thurso had always done all he could to give satisfaction to the owners. The ship had been built and manned for the trade, he had been appointed to bring the voyage to profit so Thurso determined to do what was right.

Such a story is, of course, remote from contemporary reality but it can serve to illustrate the totality of the enclosure of an ideology of the market and of the incontestable consequence of the behaviour it demands. Our perceptions of organizations constructed, manned and managed to operate in the market are already part-formed and our expectations of their performance largely set. We do what is right.

At the back of organizations are the ideological expectations of how they 'must' behave in the idea of the market and those public service organizations that were once exempt such fealty are now increasingly enclosed within the market's imperious claims. Our perceptions of the reality of organizations are already part-formed before we come to a consideration of the construction of their own particular conception.

In this sense the culture of the organization is, in some important respects, given by the ideology of the market, Corporate culture, unified and independent of sub-cultures in the organization, is defined by reference to success in the market. 'Excellent' companies have strong cultures. In Japan, in particular, that strength is reinforced:

> Japan Inc., is actually an expansion of the corporate idea on a national scale. Although this homogenization of values would not fit American culture on a national scale, we do think it has been very effective for individual companies. In fact, a strong culture has almost always been the driving force behind continuing success in American business. (Deal and Kennedy, 1982: 5)

A strong culture is business orientated, demonstrating entrepreneurial qualities that will sustain it in the market.

If corporate culture begins by reflecting the ideology of the market, those images are strengthened by the influence of leaders who are, at the level of the direction of corporate affairs, at least, likely to be actors in the real market. The formation of corporate culture further reflects those inner but contradictory qualities that are deemed to accompany success: internal unity and external competitiveness. To dwell on these seeming contradictions would be to fall into the error of contrasting cultural – or ideological – compositions with the facts, with reality. It cannot be done, we are told. Culture organizes meaning, makes our perception of reality, so we cannot break outside it in order to jeer at its inconsistencies, for, as we have been told, it does not work in a logical fashion (du Gay and Salaman, 1990; Jameson, 1991; Burrell, 1992). The several means by which the comparatively weak protest of logic is silenced includes the batteries of rhetoric, symbol, myth and the influence of economically powerful leaders. And all this is not necessarily directed at a sullen audience, predisposed to reject it; the audience itself has a culture-making capacity to form its complex experience into a coherent whole. Since what it experiences is defined by the market there is, it would seem, little likelihood of contradiction. There is evidence that the experience is reinforced by bringing the market more and more real to us. Employees engaged in production processes are reminded, under the regimes of Just-in-Time, that their performance 'is *pulled* through the factory in accordance with the configuration of final market demand' (Delbridge and Turnbull, 1992: 59). The introduction of internal markets, of chains of suppliers and users within the production process (or in the delivery of health care) makes market demand even more imminent. A study by Fuller and Smith (1991) demonstrates the systematic use of customer feedback mechanisms, including the employment of counterfeit customers or clients – 'shoppers' – to control the behaviour of employees working with customers.

The wider horizons of corporate culture

The reality behind the drive to manage culture resides in the possibility of using the evident strength of culture – its influence on behaviour and relationships in communities – so as to harness it to enhance control. The management of culture applies the influence of the market and the power of economic relationships to the reality of cultural construction. The organization, otherwise an abstract bundle of concepts, is given meaning by its members who 'think' it in ways they have developed and learned. This natural process of constructing meaning is, in cultural management, harnessed and redirected. If this process of management is successful, the meaning given to the organization by its members can be brought closer to the view that the organization or its leaders takes of itself. The result is that organizational culture is made synonymous with corporate culture.

There is a great deal to be said for this endeavour, both in terms of its assessment of social reality and of its potential for greater commitment and cooperation. The culture of communities and organizations *is* formed out of the collective experience of their members and the formation *is* influenced by leaders and the view they promulgate of history and events. There is also a long tradition stretching from Saint-Simon, through Durkheim and Elton Mayo to the contemporary change agents, that argues that the institutions of work and business are the central institutions of society and that they both are and must be encouraged to become the providers of, not only economic reward, but of meaning, fellowship and achievement. If that is the case, as it is said to be for the recipients of Japanese life-time employment, then organizations, like communities, can become the natural sources of meaning and culture. That is why it is not necessarily absurd for Deal and Kennedy (1982) to talk of the value of heroes in what might seem the most mundane environment of dough-nut or pretzel production: 'when companies make heroes out of bosses and workers – that is, when we all accept the responsi-bility of playing to a world stage – we will banish the sterility of modern organization' (p. 57). The process of incorporating, even expropriating, culture and meaning to an environment of econ-omic exchange once believed to be uncultured can extend to the claim, not only that it is a field for heroes, but that it should be seen as a cultural setting, a place for contemplation by the artist. Kanter (1985) regrets that literature had only turned to business in order to expose it: 'between Horatio Alger and the recent past we have only Willy Loman and the man in the grey flannel suit . . . But today business stories are beginning to be told for their dramatic qualities . . . The corporation is being seen as a human arena, and thus one out of which great tragedy and great comedy might be crafted' (p. 367). This presentation of the economic world as the real seat of culture is not new: licensed by a proletarian ideology it was the claim made for, first Soviet, and then Chinese 'realism' in art and literature and music. It subsequently turned out, at least in the former case, to be specious.

The case can be made that where we work is where we find meaning. That case is the ultimate root of the enhancement of corporate culture. Because culture is a reality, because it does underlie our experience of organization, it is possible to represent organizational and corporate culture as the same with no dissonance between them. If this representation succeeds then there will be no reality in the experience of employees or managers which is not encompassed by the constructed, corporate culture which is imposed upon them. Corporate culture comes to enclose our world and the meaning which we attribute to it.

There are three powerful and mutually reinforcing elements in this process. First, culture creates our perception of reality, makes the world as we see it. Next, comparisons between this construction and our experience which may seem to reveal contradictions are, we are told, impossible; all we have is what our culture provides for us. Finally, our cultural perceptions may be formed for us by the leaders, the structures and the life which our employers engage us in, by a corporate version of culture. Taken together, this amounts to an additional theoretical legitimation of already powerful processes of cultural influence. If all this were so then cultural control would be beyond the possibility of criticism and there would be no more to be said on the subject. As the next section is a criticism of corporate cultural management, that cannot be.

Summary

Before examining the effectiveness of corporate cultural management, it might be helpful to summarize the steps by which cultural development changes into cultural management.

1 The development of culture is a process natural to and inseparable from the development of communities, in which people come to share values and beliefs about their relationships and their obligations to the community. Communities are cultures.
2 These beliefs become sedimented, in communities that survive, into settled expectations, reinforced by tradition, until they are scarcely available for conscious inspection.
3 They, in turn, influence the development of procedures and structures – rules, administrative arrangements, ways of dealing with disputes – which themselves reinforce our values; our values and our experience are inter-active, mutually supporting.

4 These processes are at work in economic enterprises which, if they persist in time, become something like communities even though their purpose is economic rather than social. They develop shared values laid down in work and reinforced by habits, structures and leaders with economic power.

5 Economic leaders have an interest in the control of subordinates – including managers – in the pursuit of economic ends. Leaders come to see that the enlistment of the commitment and cooperation of subordinates might be a more effective means to the achievement of those ends than direct control.

6 The attempt – aided by what anthropologists know about the significance of culture in influencing behaviour – to influence the values of the organization is a part of that extension of control by extending the influence of its structures and leaders.

7 These influences are extended to the point that the leaders' view of the organization's culture, their values, the corporate culture, is represented as the culture itself. Corporate culture is the claim to be the organization. It is the view of the leaders transposed on to the whole.

8 If, as we are told, culture along with its accompaniment of ideology shapes our perception and experience so that contradictions are not recognized, a corporate culture cannot be challenged or criticized. If it is protected from either the practical experience of its inhabitants or the theoretical observation of outsiders, it is given added legitimation; the circle is closed.

5

WHICH CULTURE?

Managing culture, the process of bringing about a predicted state in the prevailing values and beliefs in an organization, involves two initial judgements: that the existing cultural condition is in some way unsatisfactory, and that the preferred condition, the objective of cultural change, is clearly understood. These must be the first conditions to be met before there is to be any likelihood of success in the venture: without an accurate understanding of what is wrong there can be no conception of why or in what way it should be changed, and unless there is a clear perception of what is needed there can be little chance of reaching it. Each of these judgements is difficult to make.

It is in the nature of a culture to be unperceived by those who share it and difficult to penetrate by those who do not. The accoutrements of a culture are visible enough to all but, as we are told that it is their symbolic character that is significant, that other meaning may not be apparent to those who take the architecture of buildings, the furnishing of offices, the stories and the rituals, for granted, all 'merely' a part of the way we do things here. These surface indications are visible to outsiders, signs that they are crossing a boundary into unfamiliar territory to be approached with caution because meanings have changed. For the insiders they are commonplace and unnoticed. The best explorers are well trained and equipped with maps: they are usually anthropologists. One of their own descriptions of the arduous nature of their calling was that the best way in to the culture of a remote tribe is 'to sink yourself up to the neck in the midden': rough and dedicated work. The approach approximates to participant observation, it is recommended by the Corporate Anthropology Foundation as 'the only method to allow the corporate anthropologist to make the distinctions between what people say and what they do' (Newsletter, 1.0., 1991: 6). It is a method that takes time because the researcher must become an accepted member, sometimes incognito, of the group to be observed.

Consultants adapt the understanding achieved by anthropologists but do not have as much time. It is also very difficult for them to pass themselves off as participants, except at the level at which they have been invited, the most senior level of corporate control. I know of no instance where consultants have been engaged to conduct a cultural analysis of the organization by its employees or shop stewards. Consultants may claim that they do indeed sink themselves in the midden, but the midden is invariably on the executive floor.

Barriers to analysis

The analysis of the present state of an organization's culture, preparatory to embarking upon its change, is likely to be flawed for several reasons.

It is likely to be conducted, not out of a search for truth, but because the culture has already been identified as a problem. Why not, if the insiders, who know their way around, perceive it that way; they are after all, participants and capable of observation? Their difficulty is precisely that they *are* real participants and therefore incapable of the detached observation of trained outsiders. They are also participants of a peculiar kind, remote from the realities of the 'lower participants' (the phrase is supposed to be a more neutral version of 'subordinates'). Their definition of the culture is likely to be problematic because of their own interest which, in the account of some American chief executives given by Jackall (1988), can verge upon the egocentric and the criminal. Even in the most respectable cases, it is likely to be unreliable because it will be a purposive version of culture, instrumental to the attainment of economic objectives and subject to distortion to the extent that the leaders' objectives and understanding are taken to represent the whole.

It is likely to be partial because it is not the culture itself that draws attention; it is in its nature to be unobtrusive to those that share it. Culture becomes the focus as the result of a displacement from quite different phenomena: market share, pricing, competitiveness, productive capacity, cost structure and profitability. It may be tempting to see that improvement lies in the expedient of getting everyone to work harder by the creation of a new and sophisticated version of the old team spirit. Changing the culture may seem to be a much less difficult and painful remedy than changing the market or the product or its price. It predisposes to depicting something vaguely understood as the culture as a problem: the very process that turns attention to it is likely to see it as a problem which demands change. It may result in cultural strengths, for example a strong commitment to the task by skilled workers or professionals, being seen as weaknesses.

All these incipient errors are compounded when the management's initial diagnosis is followed by the engagement of consultants whose trade is cultural change. The most rigorous and well-founded of them depend upon the market and clients who believe their problems are urgent enough to give them little time to solve them; even when they are wrong in this respect, they are not likely to be corrected by their advisers. The midden-sinking process is likely to be hasty in order to be assuring.

It is also likely to pronounce upon *the* culture of the organization and what is wrong with it before the prescription for change is delivered. Now everything that we know about cultures demonstrates that they are complex and layered. Industrial culture, itself a sub-culture in Barrie Turner's analysis, is divided and sub-divided between occupations, industries, organizations, regions and plants. Some firms with distinctive growth paths, distinctive trades or technologies, particular ownership patterns – often based on families – and strong regional associations may indeed possess unusually unified cultures (Pilkington in St Helens, Vickers Engineering and Shipbuilding in Barrow-in-Furness, Cadburys in Bournville, are examples), but even the most monolithic organizational cultures are likely to turn out to be fissured on close examination. Even that important influence on their culture, their managements, are amalgams of different values and perspectives between, say, production and marketing. The production process itself is likely to be a mare's nest of cultural differences between craft and craft, craft and process, office and shop floor, male and female. One of the reasons for the attention paid to the supervisor's role as the 'man in the middle' is that he is in the middle of several cultural currents (Child, 1982).

The first question then is which culture is to be described; but that already presupposes that there is one culture within the organization which is either believed to be the root of the trouble or is taken to be representative of the whole. There is already considerable room for misunderstanding. Error, or the potential for it, accompanies the initiation of cultural analysis in several forms:

1 *Displacement*: the attribution to cultural causes of structural weakness. It is not the values but the organization or the financial control system that is faulty.
2 *Whitewashing*: it is not the leaders but the followers, who do not understand them that must change.
3 *Scapegoating*: the attribution to the values of a particular group of responsibility for failure (such as, once upon a time, shop stewards). The fate of the scapegoat was illustrated in the painting by Burne-Jones of the goat deemed to carry the sins of the people and tethered in the desert to die.
4 *Simplification*: the belief that complex organizations mirror the unitary view taken of them by their controllers, a view that sees evidence of cultural diversity as threatening.
5 *Re-definition*: a propensity to cast strong sub-cultures as sources of weakness when they may be contributors to the cultural identity of the organization as a whole.
6 *Missionary zeal*: the belief that a complex community can be converted to a single purpose that overrides its fractional – often factional – interests and perspectives.

7 *Illusion*: a vision mistaken for reality which rests on the failure to understand an organization's culture, its history and re-inforcement by its business, traditions and management, a misunderstanding that contributes to the mistaken belief that it can change its nature without changing its setting.

These are pitfalls that can all be overcome but they do suggest that the preliminary description and analysis of culture is a difficult business and, worse, that its initiation is likely to carry built-in and disabling preconceptions. It is not so much that it cannot be carried out from within – no doubt the talent and skills exist in many HRM departments – but that managers are likely to not want to get it done. The reasons for their reluctance may themselves be cultural. Bate (1992) demonstrates that organiz-ations may possess strong cultures that predispose them to a sense of futility and pessimism:

an organizational culture can transmit to its members, a priori, the assumption that they are powerless – without them actually having to experience this at all. A state of socialized helplessness results, and this becomes an internal-ized, unquestioned 'fact'. Its reality is never tested and the resulting lack of change reinforces the initial cultural as-sumption. The culture is confirmed, and the circuit between no action and no motivation is closed. The one predicts the other (p. 229).

It may be that this pessimistic conservatism explains the enthusiasm of corporate managers for achieving change in the outlook, values, beliefs and priorities of the organization. This brings us to the second question: what is the ideal cultural state that is to be created?

Which culture is to be created?

The choice depends in part upon the perceived reason for change or the path by which change has emerged. Kanter distinguishes five explanations for corporations embarking upon change – although it is notable that her discussion is not confined to change in corporate culture (Kanter, 1985: 290–301).

'Departures from tradition' occur sometimes as the result of scattered random experiments and innovations that push the organization beyond its previous experience, enlarge the opportunities for management innovation and begin to establish a climate in which change is permissible. It might be described as an illustration of Popper's (1945) 'piecemeal social engineering' (Kanter mentions Quine's 'logical instrumentalism') which becomes an habitual attitude, and hence produces cultural change.

A 'crisis or galvanizing event' is a change in the organization's environment or within it but outside its established frameworks, a change that 'has a demand quality and seems to require a response' (Kanter, 1985: 293). The response may be facilitated by an established capacity to depart from tradition.

'Strategic decisions' are re-definitions of problems or new plans, directions and policies. They may be deliberately formulated by leaders.

Leaders, as we have seen, are credited with their own capacity to change by clearly – and repetitively, says Kanter – pointing in the direction of change and demanding its implementation. Here we move into the area of slogans and catch phrases all over the walls, the coffee mugs with the mission statements and corporate philosophies, in short, into corporate culture.

Kanter suggests that all this is likely to be ineffective unless it is supported by 'action vehicles': structures, mechanisms, processes of reward and control, that reinforce the attitudes and behaviour that is called for. The failure to achieve change, she says, 'has more to do with the lack of these kinds of integrating, institutionalizing mechanisms than with inherent problems in an innovation itself' (p. 301).

There lies a problem in the pursuit of cultural change: it is difficult to determine whether the mechanistic supports for change would have been sufficient to bring it about without the hyperbolic advertisement of its necessity. It raises a fundamental question of the nature of the change that is required: whether it is to be a change in culture or a change in the behaviour of the organization's employees. Four out of the five of Kanter's forces for change are material rather than inspirational, and they are important because they are likely to change behaviour in response to a discernible shift in the environment within which people have to operate. We do not have to enter into a discussion of the old debate about whether people are materially determined by their surroundings or are free agents exercising choice to acknowledge that we at least take our surroundings into account in judging appropriate behaviour. It is an adaptive necessity without which our survival becomes a matter of doubt and uncertainty. Utilitarian philosophy and individual psychology agree that we tend to behave in a way that will be rewarded and not so as to incur punishment and deprivation – although we may be capable of more, and more unpredictable, choices than rats in mazes. Performance-related reward schemes, codes of conduct, disciplinary rules, promotion, total quality management (TQM) programmes and the rest of the apparatus of organizational life rests on these elementary assumptions. We do, within limits, what we learn is expected of us and eschew, for the most part, what is proscribed. Even in normative, 'professional' organizations, we are capable of finely tuned responses to changes in the wind. The performance of universities is increasingly evaluated in terms of their research performance rather than their teaching. Universities, in their turn, evaluate and promote members of academic staff by reference to their record of publication. It becomes immediately apparent that short 'papers' are more economical and effective in the amassing of points for promotion or tenure than the publication of books. The optimum length of papers becomes a matter of precise calculation. Behaviour in universities is at least as rationally conditioned by the structure as is the behaviour of employees in factories. There are exceptions, as you may have noticed. Professor Roy Wilky once remarked of this control system, 'poor Wittgenstein; only two short books in the whole of his career'.

But, for the most part, behaviour is easier to change than values or culture. And, for the most part, change in behaviour is sufficient for organizational purposes. 'Resigned behavioural compliance' which brings cash-point operators in supermarkets or airline passenger staff to smile is good enough for operational purposes and it is relatively easy to achieve. What corporate cultural management requires, as we have seen, is sincerity or authenticity in the performance.

Behavioural compliance is achievable and it may accrete, in

time, to create cultural formations, systems of value and belief that reflect and support behaviour that was sustained to begin with for more material reasons. In circumstances in which behaviour is controlled by constraint and coercion and also reinforced by symbolic means, the process of cultural construction may be accomplished quite quickly. Recruits to the armed services, the police force or the medical profession are regularly moulded to patterns of 'acceptable' behaviour and then to a certain commonality of attitudes and meanings by a combination of reward, deprivation and the symbolic construction of outlook. This rapid transmission of compliance and understanding is accomplished in these cases by the induction of recruits to established organizations with identifiable cultures and determined 'ways of doing things here'. Enculturation is the result of the application of power, reflected in systematic structures and encoded in configurations of shared meanings. This is essentially different from the choice of a new culture to be pursued because of a perceived need to bring about harmony of purpose in an integrated and sincere network of beliefs and values.

In many cases of cultural management, the change to a new culture is pursued either in isolation from other changes or as the first objective from which all other change will follow. The new culture, almost by definition, is isolated and made paramount over other more mundane and structural matters. The aim is often a culture of participation which will release energy and cooperation in the pursuit of the new corporate mission. But participation and cooperation seem incompatible with conflict. Because there are not supposed to be any factional rivalries their expression is discouraged or avoided; it is likely to present antagonistic obstacles to the pursuit of a consensus of values.

Thus Deal and Kennedy (1982) warn against the naivety of the belief that structural change will be sufficient in improving corporate performance, that reshuffling the marketing department or installing a new budgeting procedure will produce necessary improvement. The hidden danger is that such peripheral change will run into cultural barriers, antagonize employees, cause confusion and insecurity. Real or meaningful change involves cultural transformation: managers contemplating it 'should recognise that . . . they will have to wrestle with their company's culture' (p. 159). They acknowledge that cultural change can take years to accomplish.

One form of the question, 'which culture?' is whether it is culture or structure that should change. The warning that structural change unsupported by cultural transformation will run into trouble is, no doubt, sensible enough unless we think that the trouble is better faced than avoided. Conflict and its avoidance is part of the established tradition of human relations policies and has earned itself criticism for its unreality (Coser, 1956; Dahrendorf, 1959; Fox, 1966). The cultural emanation of human relations is similarly open to the charge that its pursuit of changed attitudes by participative methods is concerned to produce the appearance of peace, reinforced this time by a coercive appeal to the market rather than the more pious expression of goodwill. Perhaps it would be better – that is, more expedient – as well as more honest to face the turmoil of dealing with antagonism, confusion and insecurity following structural change than to conceal those natural responses in programmes of cultural wall-papering. Such a choice would, however, be painful in practice and a recognition that the corporate identity conceals differences of interest and power.

The option for cultural change is, as we have seen, sometimes presented as an alternative to structural change, sometimes as a necessary accompaniment to it. As an accompaniment, the case carries some conviction, despite the dangers of conflict camouflage that attend it; as an alternative it is likely to be disastrous. Cultural change that is not reinforced by material change in structure, reward systems, precept and policy is likely to be seen as unreal and any adjustment to be temporary. The necessity for reinforcement is a consistent theme in the more reliable literature (Schein, 1985; Smith and Peterson, 1988). A case that illustrates the symbiosis between the two is provided by the valuable study of the Cadbury experience (Smith et al., 1990).

The authors describe a comprehensive programme of change involving capital investment, rationalization and changed working practices, attributing it, in part, to the reshaping of corporate culture through the use of new concepts and symbols which served to focus on targets and practices. Note that, at the start of this account, culture is related and perhaps validated by specific and observable outcomes. They go on to say that the new culture was 'complementary to the restructuring of the existing bases of entrenched power by the leading managers behind the trans-formation' (Smith et al., 1990: 339). The relevance of the distribution of power meant that conflicts of interest were revealed rather than suppressed, a process in which 'certain groups suffer not only disturbance but often an economic loss and/or one of relative status . . . as a result, the transformation at Cadburys proceeded through confrontation between management and organized labour, as well as engendering conflict between functional groups within management' (p. 340).

Successful transformation depended upon forethought and careful planning and involved 'the interplay of structures, relationships and cognitive frameworks' (p. 341). The basic feature of organizational life, we are told, is that 'structures frame action and action itself reframes structure' (p. 342).

The final answer to the question, 'which culture is to be chosen as a replacement for the old?' is that it must be the wrong question. In that form, the question is subsumed under one of three approaches to organizational change:

1 A change in the organizational culture is sufficient in itself: from it all that is necessary will follow.
2 Cultural change must precede structural change which will otherwise be negated by hostility born of old values.
3 Cultural change or at least a version of it – the reshaping of cognitive frameworks – must be woven into the planned change in structure and power relationships.

The first, simplistic approach is most likely to change corporate culture but not to influence the beliefs and values of subordinates or the security of established sub-cultures. The second is more realistic but it runs the risk of attempting to head off, to suppress or ignore differences of interest, largely because they are not likely to be apparent and open until structural changes are set in place. At that point the fragility of cultural changes that are believed to have been made will be revealed. The risk of this happening is compounded by an attitude to conflict that is endemic in the movement for cultural change which, by its inception, history and definition, sees the expression of conflict

61

as inimical to organizational health: cultural management is soaked in the belief in harmony. The third more complex approach escapes these difficulties by the acknowledgement that structure is itself an influence upon values which are also related to interests, often entrenched by cultural defences in groups and functions, many of them within the ranks of management. Rather than attempting to instil new corporate values through the techniques of communication and training, it faces the consequence of disturbance and conflict and, instead of the facile achievement of apparent consensus, it tackles the problems of change in understanding by rational means.

All this is much more difficult and is likely to be attended by evidence of what seems to be the opposite of what is being pursued – trouble and dissent. That is sufficient explanation for the enthusiasm for corporate cultural change. This is in harmony with a view which sees management, British management in particular, as consistent in the pursuit of insulation from the difficult realities of controlling labour (or managers) by the promotion of protective intermediaries – sub-contractors, foremen, personnel departments, employers associations (Anthony, 1986). Cultural management can be seen, in that context, as the last great escape from difficulty and responsibility.

This is in part an explanation for the postponed question, why is cultural management so enthusiastically pursued against the evidence of its limitations? It offers the advantages of comparative ease, totality of control and escape from responsibility for subsequent failure. But its greatest appeal may lie in the completion of the separation of the controllers of organizations from their environment.

The choice of the culture sought by corporate managers, the answer to the question, 'which culture?', may be determined by their own search for security. If corporate culture is seen simply as the expression of the managerial sub-culture, then it becomes apparent that it encloses its members and cocoons members in a singularity of meaning which is beyond objection or dissent. One of the functions of corporate culture and one of the reasons for its pursuit is the comfortable isolation that it provides. While isolated from the complexities of reality, it interprets reality in terms of its own unity, places the complex association of men and women engaged by merely economic contract and instrumental attachment in an almost spiritual bond dedicated to goals generally identified as of central significance to society. Corporate versions of culture impose upon fissured organizational culture their own comforting unity. They convert the mundane into the missionary and promise to provide a life purpose for all, identifying the managers as the life-givers. The narratives of cultural excellence, the stories of cultural transformation, feature their leaders as heroes – visionary leaders with charismatic qualities who can convert the unfaithful. The means at their disposal transcend the merely rational methods of the old and unsuccessful managers; they include the magical and the symbolic, powerful icons once available only to priesthoods. They are told, not only that they are the stuff of legends, but how to write their own legends.

They are also told how, once legends are established, they are beyond the risk of refutation. The old – one is tempted to say, real – legendary heroes, Achilles, Siegfreid, King Arthur, were kept within the comprehension and sympathy of the rest of us because they were vulnerable. The new corporate heroes have no heels. They have been given the secret of the inner logic of cultural control, that it transcends contradiction. Cultural protection from refutation is itself protected (as we saw in Chapter 3) by the unchallengable sovereignty of the idea of the market which has itself turned into a paramount concern with the production of images rather than commodities (Jameson, 1991); 'in the contemporary world . . . the appearance of things, their simulation via the media, especially television, can come to seem more significant than reality' (Turner, 1992). Layer upon layer of obfuscation has to be penetrated before we come to the impenetrable protection of culture's widely acclaimed ability to deal with the painful contradictions between its metaphors and our harsh experience.

The real function of corporate culture is that it protects those it encloses from reality. The dangers of that enclosure, of the management of culture to those who should be managing organizations, is the next concern.

6

THE THREAT TO
MANAGEMENT: SCHIZOPHRENIA

We have suggested that to regard cultural change as alternative to or even as necessarily proceeding before adjustments in structure and power, is dangerously misleading. Let us look at the nature of this danger for managers.

The argument for the precedence of culture over structure takes a prescriptive form. It emerges in the current criticism of rational systems, characterized by Morgan (1986) as the machine metaphor of organizations. The rational systems model is generally held to be dehumanizing, unadaptive to change in the environment, productive of sectional rivalry, inflexible, alienating, remote, bureaucratic and prone to induce passivity, apathy or downright hostility among subordinates. The slogan 'the one best way' has turned out to be an epitaph for Fordism in a post-Fordist world. Rational systems and centralism are, we are told, no longer appropriate to conditions of uncertainty, of segmented market change and new technology. The criticism is followed by prescriptions for new organizations which *should* become leaner, flatter, more decentralized and entrepreneurial. It may seem odd that the examples of the new excellence include organizations like McDonalds, Nissan, Toyota, which, in many respects, seem to represent the metaphor of the machine.

A comparison with the observation of such work organizations and the experience of their workers suggests that, in two senses, there is something unreal about these accounts of production and administrative processes. In the first place, control over be-haviour – often enhanced to an unprecedented degree – seems to be a common feature of many successful organizations. In the second, quite a lot of them seem to have been remarkably adaptive: the Civil Service, the Army, the BBC, the banks, Marks & Spencer, Unilever – all have shown considerable staying power in a changing world without abandoning their systematic methods of management and control. 'Any industrial corpor-ation, such as IBM or General Electric, that has survived the last fifty years of social change in the United States has done so through a process of self-transformation and not through the continuation of original organizational patterns' and their charac-teristic 'ultrastability' is due to the learning and innovating capacity demonstrated by complex, formal social organizations (Cadwallader, 1966: 397). The apparatus of systematic control and central direction is not necessarily the cause of atrophy and degeneration. One of the operational problems in sustaining the current attack on bureaucracy is just how much of a machine has to be present to justify the label of the machine metaphor to an organization.

In other words, some of the assault on rational systems and structure is just a little, shall we say, theoretical. The actual practice of management may continue to celebrate the rational pursuit of goals supported by an apparatus of controls. The very strength of the attack upon rational systems and structure and the catalogue of alleged disasters to which it has given rise is testimony to their persistent, though allegedly dire, influence. The attack amounts to a description of behaviour and an appeal that it should stop, supported by some very general accounts of 'best practice' meant to suggest that the appeal has had some success. At least, we may conclude, managers were sunk in these wicked ways until the day before yesterday when some of them were won over to the new ways of managing. If that is the case, the influence of systems and structures must have been huge and only very recently diminished. And if so recent, whatever the extent of the reduction, its effects would hardly be felt yet. If so, it is the managerial world of systems, structures and controls that we must still reckon with as a prime influence upon behaviour in organizations.

The argument that systematic management, organizations like machines, is still the characteristic pattern does not have to be laboured; the evidence lies all around us from burger bars to the manufacture of our televisions and word processors. The debate is whether this state of affairs should continue. Cultural management presents an alternative which, it is claimed, would unify meanings and purposes and release previously restricted energy. So it might, but the immediate problem is in the consequences of the coexistence of these two opposed approaches. The problem is an acute one for the managers who have to operate the structures while being induced to see simple, unstructured visions.

The contradiction between the practice in which managers engage and the new culture which they must accept is presented in its sharpest and most visible form in any of the management development programmes that are taking place in local authorities, banks, building societies and manufacturing companies at this moment. From some, often mysterious, source the message and the mission comes to the chief executive and quickly infects human resource services who begin to set it cascading down those hierarchies soon, it seems, to be dismantled. Layers of managers, cohort after cohort, are marched in to be given the blessing of the priests and sent out like missionaries to spread the new faith. It is not a call to action because action unsupported by faith will not suffice any longer. If all are to be empowered all must have the faith to be free. Managers must become leaders but their subordinates are now lower participants, participating in the new faith and they too must be leaders. The organization – unfortunately the word cannot yet be avoided – is to become a New Model Army, its muskets directed by its faith.

The original New Model Army fought and triumphed, defeated the King, endured hardship – often without pay – and came to see that its radical mission had been abandoned by its generals, if they had ever shared it. At Burford, Cromwell confronted his Army and executed two representative soldiers drawn by lot.

The parallel with the new management is not intended to suggest that managers are likely to become mutinous or revolutionary (although that prediction has been seriously made in some quarters). Managers are likely to get on with their work because they are rewarded for it and because they are not given to abstract political or philosophical speculation. It might be observed that speculation of a particularly abstract sort is precisely what they are now being encouraged to engage in but there is no prospect that it is likely to take any radical direction. The problem is, rather, that it is not likely to take any direction at all.

To return to our managerial cohorts. On being introduced to heady exhortations to greatness such as, 'if values are the soul of the culture, then heroes personify those values and epitomize the strength of the organization . . . the hero is the great motivator, the magician' (Deal and Kennedy, 1982: 37), what are they actually supposed to do? The purpose of their transcendental training experiences is to convert them between leaving the bank or the factory and returning to it. And what they have left behind and will return to, for the most part, is a centralized, fairly efficient, bureaucratic structure. It is a structure for which they have been recruited, which has provided them with experience from which they have learned in action and the values and expectations in action they have come to understand. And when they get back to it after their short metaphysical trip, if they are in any understandable doubt about priorities for action, they will be reminded by new sets of controls – set up while they were away and intended to monitor their own evangelical conversion to the new culture – that it is the bureaucracy that continues to rule.

Management as acting

In one sense this is no special problem for managers. Contradictory demands from a plurality of purposes forms their usual environment to the extent that their function has been described as mediation between them. In the ordinary circumstances of their work they constantly shift and adjust to conflicting roles that they are required to play. So adept do they become that a variety of commentators from quite different perspectives see them as actors. Jackall (1988) describes effective managers as good actors. MacIntyre (1981) sets out to undermine their credibility and their pretension to authority: 'the most effective bureaucrat is the best actor' (p. 102). Mangham (1987) analyses relationship between senior managers in terms of the performance of *commedia dell'arte*. The explanation, increasingly frequent and persuasive, of the importance of political relationships in the management process tends also to emphasize skills of dissembling and rhetorical performance. If histrionic skill is their stock in trade, why should the acquisition of new values in corporate cultures present any difficulty for them even if it does contradict their experience of reality?

The question raises some issues about the nature of acting, its relationship to reality and the meaning of authenticity in performance. These may seem remote from the real business of managers, but, if the real business of managers is defined in cultural terms, the relationship becomes much more immediate.

An actor's performance has to be convincing if it is to be effective, but it remains a performance. The explanations of the ways in which this feat is accomplished include the closely observed, surface replication of features and behaviour, witness on the one hand Olivier's crippled gait as Richard the Third, and on the other hand, the deeper absorption into the truth of a character – the actor who lives his performance on and off the stage. They are different approaches to the achievement of authenticity, a totally convincing performance. We should remember, incidentally, that whatever such theatrical events are believed to do for the audience, there has always existed a view that they are very bad for the actors who must 'suffer the attenuation of selfhood that results from impersonation' (Trilling, 1974: 64). This is a warning of which managers might take heed.

The authentic performance depends upon a script, direction and acting all brought together in the artificial surroundings of a theatre. The script determines authenticity to a large extent but it is well known that a poor script can be salvaged by good actors. The influence of the director is relatively modern but has assumed increasing importance, to the extent that actors are now regarded as subordinate to the director's sometimes eccentric reading of the script. One view sees the emergence of the director as a repressive force that reduces actors to slavery and, in reaction to this, 'new forms of theatre reduce the control of the director by emphasising improvization and group authorship' (Connor, 1989: 136) – a movement for greater participation, it would seem.

The artificiality of the theatre, its very 'theatricality' has always presented a problem in the pursuit of authenticity. In the twentieth century the problem of self-conscious artificiality has been tackled by exposure, by the deconstruction of the setting of the theatre in absurdist drama which refuses to engage in drama at all or by setting the play – sometimes unscripted – outside the theatre.

If managers are actors, how is their performance to be related to these other important elements in theatre? Is there a script and, if there is, who writes it? Who directs the performance? Performance may, as in the theatre, be transitory or continuous, but it cannot take place – at least, not for long – without the presence of an audience, otherwise there can surely be no judgement of the extent to which authenticity has been achieved. Who, then, is the audience?

These entirely superficial questions remind us that we may be wasting our time in pressing the analogy between managing and acting, that it may merely be another useful metaphor but no more. But the frequency with which the comparison is made, the relevance of and the very term used in 'role theory' to account for managerial behaviour, and the common observation that managers really do have to provide convincing performances all suggest that there is some truth in it. Managers *are* performers seeking to exercise control over the feelings and responses of others. And we can agree that their performance is subject to direction by others exercising great influence over how their parts are to be played in terms of style and intention. And the script? Perhaps there are no authors, but Mangham (1987) reminds us that *commedia dell'arte* needed none: brief descriptions of the parts were pinned up in the wings and the actors extemporized their performances in well-known plots. In this sense, Mangham demonstrates that the personnel director and the marketing director know their parts and play them subject to the minor irregularities of interaction.

69

But the audience, who is the audience? Who determines authenticity?

There are dramatic performances, or something very like them, without an audience and with no theatre. The enactment of rituals in communities and tribes might involve all their members; early comedy and tragedy were both linked to annual festivals, Christian or pagan and to religious rite. Monastic observances involve the whole religious community. Games are dramas of a kind (the etymological connection between 'play' as action, exercise or movement and 'play' as mimic action and, thence, as theatrical performance is clearly established in *The Shorter Oxford English Dictionary*) and they were, before the days of spectator sports, intended for the players, not the audience. In this sense, the absence of an audience does not vitiate the perception of managers as actors. In rituals, rites, games and organizations, authenticity is conferred by the players' performance of their roles. Let us call this kind of drama without the audience auto-authenticizing theatre and the performance it requires auto-authentic.

The performance also requires a script but it need not be lengthy or verbatim: as we have seen, in *commedia dell'arte*, it is the merest outline of the plot and the roles to be taken by the players. The broad outline of the managerial script is provided by the underlying ideology of the market for entrepreneurial concerns, of service provision for government agencies, or of normative values for professional groups. The outlines are crystallized and laid down into more behavioural values and rules and expectations in the formation of organizational cultures. The rest is extemporization, adaptation to the unscripted performance of the other players.

The other ingredient in the drama is direction. Who are the directors? We cannot answer that the directors are managers because the managers are the players. It is of little use to rely on the simple and unhelpful distinction between top managers and the rest – despite the attractive identification of boardroom and theatrical control in the one word, 'director'. We have suggested that direction comes from others who exercise great influence on how the various parts are to be played in terms of style and intention. This is the point at which the leaders, heroes, founders

70

and charismatic personalities who are so frequently featured in the popular criticism of the management drama enter. We shall leave them for consideration in the next section.

We have now assembled all the contributors to an auto-authentic performance: the actors, the script and the director. What determines authenticity?

The concept of authenticity is extraordinarily complex for a term that is associated with truth, simplicity and genuineness: 'it is a word of ominous import' (Trilling, 1974: 93). It occasions metaphysical speculation upon the nature of being and existentialist examination of the identity of the self. In the world of art and museums, it means the original as against the copy and that suggests that there is something vulnerable about it. The idea of the self is frequently seen as threatened: by the fall from grace, by society, by market capitalism; innocence threatened by sophistication; the authenticity of nature corrupted. Authenticity is simple, but it seems extraordinarily difficult to achieve and, if attained, very easily lost. In theatrical performance, the authentic is true and convincing; more than believable, it is believed – by the audience, of course, but in our peculiar performance of the auto-authentic it is largely the players who must be convinced, as they are in the repetitions of rites and rituals. For managers there are special difficulties. The script may present no great problem: it encloses them in an ideological framework, reinforced by an organizational culture to which they have become conditioned. Problems of contradictions with 'reality' that may face them from time to time are the kind that culture functions to deal with – it is, after all, the capacity for cultural construction of reality that gives cultural management its particular appeal. This is the play in which they are meant to act. It is the direction of the script that makes it unrecognizable and its performance inauthentic. It is the attempt to substitute for the organizational culture with which managers are perfectly familiar (familiarity is too distant a term for the relationship, the organizational culture is *theirs*) a corporate culture that is foreign to them, inauthentic.

The breakdown in dramatic performance caused by dissonance is described by Hopfl (1991) as 'corpsing' – 'what happens when an actor loses his/her place in the script, dries, is unable to continue, no longer believes in the play, sees the audience

71

watching and waiting, freezes to the spot, cannot sustain the illusion'. She argues that the attempt to impose culturally managed performances of consensus and organizational commitment on the dissonant experience of managers is similarly treated as an 'offence against decorum'. What this means for managers asked to take part in the corporate drama if they are unable to sustain a coherent commitment within the corporate definition of reality is that they 'corpse', they 'see the play for what it is and experience the "shock of recognition"'. She goes on to describe the result when two out of three senior managers invited to contribute to a workshop on 'Your future with our Company' were sacked the day before it began.

Inauthentic management

The strangeness of the disparity between managers' experience of cultural reality and the presentations of corporate culture which they are required to believe, is almost impossible to penetrate because all attempts at cultural control – the grandiose political examples are known to us all in recent history – are accompanied by their self-supporting censorships and apparatus for the suppression of criticism. One cannot find out what goes on in the training and communication sessions without being a part of them and in that case one cannot speak of the experience. Unless, in the very privileged position of a visitor who has been invited to help by cultural managers who have mistaken a critic for an ally, the curtain is momentarily lifted. Here is such an account provided by an occasional visitor to events intended to mould new corporate cultures:

> Outside the forum of the management course and safely apart from the Director of Human Resource Strategy, when the outsider asks empty questions like, 'and how are things in the Company?' managers answer with candour and wit. Things haven't changed at all and are not likely to do so. Asked in syndicates, more purposefully, to provide metaphors (pace Morgan) for how they see their slim, entrepreneurial, mission driven companies, they bring back vivid descriptions of elephants, cart horses, dinosaurs, tanks,

hearses. More seriously still, they report that their performance is measured by the old standards of behaviour, that
there is a dichotomy between the real expectations of what
they must do and the simple new language that they have
been quickly taught to acquire. They learn to talk culture and
are otherwise unscathed.

The new heroes are to be washed in the cascades of communication where they will learn to overturn the bureaucracies which
have produced them and which will monitor their conversion
when they return to their offices and factories. Such a process
opens up a dangerous rift between reality and experience on a
greater scale than the kind that culture is supposed to be so adept
at reconciling. It is a contradiction between working life, already
reinforced and protected from the more ephemeral experiences
of contradiction by a rooted working culture, and the sense that
corporate employers seem to demand its managers to make of it.
It is also likely to contradict the accumulated experience, the
history, that the working organization has enshrined in its
culture. The danger from the past and what it teaches the
managers of how they must deal with the present is recognized
by some of the cultural managers of change: 'organizational change
consists in part of a series of emerging constructions of reality, including
revision of the past, to correspond to the requisites of new players and new
demands, Organizational history *does* need to be rewritten to
permit events to move on' (Kanter, 1985: 287–8, emphasis in
original).

The deliberate separation from reality, as it has been moulded
by the organization's history, from the interpretation of it
required by its managers, would seem to be a dangerous process.
The danger would seem to be compounded when the organization's history, represented in its culture and shared by its
inhabitants, has to be recast to facilitate the current leader's
conception of its future. There are several risks involved.

Despite what we know of the essential subjectivity of 'knowledge', of the way our perceptions are influenced by cultural
considerations, these considerations must seem arcane to all but
philosophers, as you may have observed. The belief that knowledge is real and reliable, rooted in tests for objectivity and truth

73

and established and trustworthy methods of prediction, is widespread and necessary. We must trust our perception of the environment and our methods of dealing with the data our senses give us, along with our powers of reasoning, whatever philosophers tell us, because we can do no other. This trust has been made the foundation of commercial and administrative organizations as an extension of the natural and applied sciences and, just as bridges built on sound engineering principles do not, for the most part, fall down, neither do organizations frequently collapse – and when they do, we can often blame negligence, error or malpractice. Our experience of work therefore reinforces our basic empirical faith in our senses and our ability to reason: we tend to believe what we see and what works. To be told that our collective and shared understandings, reinforced in the ways we are required to work, are unreliable and that our collective memory of events and our history is mistaken is unsettling.

Some kind of danger may be inherent in the employment situation itself. One way of explaining this is to describe the organization and its managers as auto-authenticating, dependent upon no response external to itself, the organization has no audience to verify its performance. Organizations are commonly believed to be subject only to the market's judgement of their performance, but even that arbitor can be unreliable and subject to control by the organization. For the rest there is a dangerous absence of external control and little independent criticism accompanying a large accumulation of power, some of it wielded by the very maverick heroes we are being told to admire. Some solutions to this perceived problem, not always simply directed at the redistribution of economic resources as in socialist proposals, encouraged the radical redistribution of management power, by the appointment of worker directors. Those that have been tried have not been successful. Some sociologists were optimistic about a general change in the pattern of work and its control, because improvement in productivity and education would diminish differences in interest and ideology (Bell, 1961; Halmos, 1965) or because changes in processes of production and control would reduce alienation (Blauner, 1964). Others believed that the reduced centrality and importance of work itself and the evidence of an instrumental attitude to it would reduce the

74

dominance of work and, consequently, the imbalance of power enjoyed by its controllers (Dahrendorf, 1959; Goldthorpe et al., 1968). That expectation is, of course, opposed by the strategies of cultural control we are discussing: it is their intention to make work more, not less central.

Those strategies are likely to exaggerate a tendency to enclose organizational members more thoroughly in their work setting and to separate them from any independent perception of reality. The dangers are greater for managers who have to continue to operate the apparatus of control while not only behaving as though, but believing that, it has been dismantled.

Separation from reality: alienation, anomie and scepticism

There are several names for the disorders attending personal divorce from reality.

The most familiar is alienation, a term used so variously as to have lost a great deal of utility. The notion of separation and loss conveyed by the word is present in the two traditions in which it is used; the social and economic on the one hand, and the psychological on the other. The first tradition is associated with Marx and concerns the damage done to the worker and thence to society by capitalist relations of production and exchange. Schisms within this tradition seek to de-politicize the argument by attributing the causes of alienation to technology rather than capitalism. The psychological usage goes back to the earlier description of insanity as 'alienation' and descriptions of psychiatrists as 'alienists'. Baxter (1982) suggests that a rejuvenation of the psychological attributes of the term avoids 'a specific ethical or political approach to the worth of work and instead permits an exploration of its value in, or indifference towards, establishing a personal authenticity' (p. 70).

'Anomie' denotes a condition related to the latter usage. The term comes from the Greek and it meant a condition of lawlessness in which the law is defined in the broadest sense as the canons and norms of the society in which the individual lives. Anomie is a condition of moral lawlessness. Its current usage is associated with the work of Durkheim who believed it was the cause of social disorder. In terms of our present concern it might not be stretching meaning too far to suggest that anomie is the condition in which the person is outside moral and therefore cultural control.

Three elements seem to be present in these accounts of separation from relationship with society: economic deprivation; psychological deprivation – or lack of the potential for self-actualization; moral disassociation. The first was the engine for socialist programmes of revolution or reform and, quite apart from its current discrediting in the regimes of Eastern Europe, it showed little success in improving the personal condition of the worker or his relationship to society. Capitalist societies may or may not turn out to solve problems of poverty – if they do, they may have to succeed beyond their own borders to survive – but it is in the realms of the psychological and the moral that some critics see the greatest crisis. The current concern with cultural management could be interpreted as the last great gamble in this respect, in which the free market solves its problems of relationship with people by seeking to enclose them completely within its own material ethos. Our argument here is that the movement in this direction sets out to provide and control meaning as an instrumental means for purely market advantage. That does not necessarily invalidate any claims that may accompany the case for the cultural management of pretzel production, that it will also produce a life purpose for happier pretzel workers, but we are entitled to express some scepticism on the matter.

Scepticism is exactly what many managers and employees express about programmes of cultural management – once they escape from the requirements of behavioural compliance – induced, as we have noted, by quite uncultural and old-fashioned methods of control. The new Shell philosophy was greeted with scepticism, early and late, as we saw in Chapter 1. In one of the latest studies, a life assurance company is described as setting out on the familiar path: the flattening of the hierarchy – achieved partly by redundancy, resignation and early retirement, reorganization into team based production, and greater employee participation, all contributing to a new ethos and greater identification with the company. The methods were also familiar:

glossy presentations to successive cohorts of staff, emphasis on team spirit and the requirement that the converts should 'spread the word' and disseminate the new image, cascading responsibility. The comments were equally familiar:

'You get the "we're all part of a team" at the big production meeting and when you get back to work the following morning things are just the same as they always were.'

'They can see that they're being patronised . . . Making them feel part of a team when really, everyone's here to do a job of work and if you don't, certain consequences follow. In a way I feel it's cosmetic.'

[The researchers comment that] 'clearly there was more than a degree of scepticism about the Team Building Programme' [and that it extended from the subordinate staff] 'into the ranks of lower and middle management'. (Kerfoot and Knights, 1992).

Scepticism can be seen as a product or an accompaniment of the kinds of separation that we have been discussing:

Scepticism, the arch-indifference, is the estrangement of those disinterested in present values, work ethics, cultural norms, and ideologies. It is possible to see the significance of role-playing for the estranged sceptic. Conventionally, it is understood as the act of an individual who desires a form of separation from the world as protection from personal involvement. (Baxter, 1982: 98)

Baxter goes on to suggest that, on the other hand, it may be the only means for the sceptic to retain contact with the world, by adopting and discarding different roles, each of them transitory and ephemeral.

All managers are actors and likely to be protected by some measure of scepticism from their auto-authentic performance. Their detachment from reality, I suggest, is likely to be greater when the values presented to them for acceptance are totally at odds with their experience of reality. There is a danger of this state of affairs coming about as the result of corporate cultures being imposed upon managers who have to live and work by reference to working rules that are contradicted by the values the managers are ostensibly required to accept. It is managers rather than subordinate employees who are likely to suffer most from this impasse because the latter are less enclosed within the pursuit of corporate goals, less responsible in every way for their achievement and less personally identified with their pursuit. Subordinates also enjoy the protection of membership of alternative cultures, more segmented involvement in the organization's culture and a more instrumental outlook on their work. For managers the result of a serious deviation of their values in work from the values espoused by their organization is more serious. Exposure to this fundamental contradiction, repeatedly illuminated for them in the difference between what they know they are supposed to do and what they are told they are supposed to believe, is likely to drive them from scepticism to cynicism.

Summary

The purpose of our excursion to the theatre was to demonstrate the fragility, the unreality of the manager's role. The manager must always act, in more senses than one. The rest of us believe in the performance because it has economic and social consequences supported by values that we share. Managed organizations are part of our culture. There is a sense in which corporate culture stretches credulity and requires managers to do more than perform, to believe in visions that are not compatible with their experience.

The serious pursuit of corporate culture along the lines that are currently recommended, its continued separation from the structural realities in which managers have to live and work, represents the attempt to require them to live in an unreal world. It may be that this is the real purpose of programmes of corporate cultural control, to detach the corporate organization and the view it takes of itself from uncomfortable comparison with reality, to secure it in auto-authentic applause. If so, to return to our theatrical metaphor, managers may now be required to act in a theatre of the absurd in which the playhouse of the market has been abandoned. If that is not the case then either the world or the managers will have to give. In the latter case the result is likely to be managerial schizophrenia; in the former, organizational chaos. The only hope is that the pursuit of the management of corporate culture will either be abandoned or that it will be unsuccessful. There might be one other ground for optimism: that even the leaders who promote it do not believe their own pronouncements. It is to our leaders that we now turn.

7

THE THREAT TO
LEADERSHIP: ISOLATION

A leader can be regarded as someone whose influence over others resides in the power of the office or in personal qualities possessed or attributed by others. A great deal of the attention to leadership in organizations has associated it with management and, therefore, with deployment of the power of office. There are particular reasons why we should 'maintain a distinction between the leader who is in a leadership position and who has power and authority vested in his or her office, and leadership as an influence process which is more than the exercise of power and authority' (Bryman, 1986: 4). The exercise of the power of office is a matter of management and administration; the excess, left over after the power of office, is largely a matter of culture and, therefore, our particular concern.

Once again, the distinction is not precise. The influence of power is legitimated by those subordinated to it in a relationship of authority; it is vested in the superior by the subordinate. Those deemed to be wielding legitimate power can influence the behaviour of others to an extent that seems to require the denial of their moral standards, as the notorious conclusions of Milgram's experiments seemed to demonstrate. But the difference between coercive and persuasive influence is real and is the explanation for the attention given to the influence of leadership upon organizational culture. Much of that attention concerns the leader's ability to create and influence meaning: 'the leader is the person who actively moulds the organization's image for both internal and external consumption and who suffuses it with a sense of direction' (Bryman, 1986:185). The legendary tales of Peters and Waterman, Deal and Kennedy and the rest are full of transformations in performance consequent upon transformations in meaning wrought by leaders. It is their ability to change what we mean and what is meaningful to us that is said to make them into heroes and distinguishes them from the ordinary run of mortals and managers, thus the association of leadership with charismatic qualities.

This neo-romantic movement is not so much a mistake as an exaggeration of the personal influence of the leader. It runs into problems, particularly in management education and development, about succession; hence Deal and Kennedy's reassurance that heroes are not *too* different from the rest of us to make it impossible to reproduce them. It has to a large extent failed to find support in the considerable body of research devoted to the discovery of the essence of leadership over a period of some seventy years 'during which researchers into leadership acted as though they were medieval alchemists in search of the philosophers' stone' (Smith and Peterson, 1988: 11). That their disappointment has not dimmed the interest in leadership is one of the mysteries we are trying to unravel.

One of the explanations is that the clients of the study of leadership and its influence on culture are leaders, or at least the organizations that reflect the leaders' opinion of their significance. Quite apart from the frustrated search for the quintessential leader, a large part of the direction of that search has been from within the organization under the influence of the leader. Even before we reach the attribution of extraordinary powers to leaders, they are frequently seen as monarchical in their power and in their representative capacity. In many cases the leader is identified with the organization and the organization is personified in its leader.

Personification and representation have great utility in handling the abstract concept of organization, but it is the utility of metaphor not of reality. To understand the utility of representation we must see the leader as symbolizing it for other people; as in the case of the monarchy. The Queen stands for the nation but is not the same as it and cannot be identified with it or with the behaviour of its politicians and citizens. There is a hieratic element in leadership which associates it with magical power and distances it from mundane responsibility. There is a propensity in us to see leaders – particularly of the colourful variety – as unreal, legendary figures. But it is not what they do to the organization so much as what part of its meaning they represent to outsiders that gives them this mysterious quality. In other words, leaders have both an inside and an outside function.

Another way of putting this is to say that leaders can be understood as standing not so much at the apex of the organization but at its boundary, representing it both to those lower participant employees who are only partially enclosed by it, and to those entirely outside it. They also straddle the boundary in the sense that they often seem to represent the external environment, to bring a sharp, clear picture of the world to bear upon the organization; they combine the 'outsider's objective view of their firms with the credibility and power base usually associated with insiders' (Kotter and Heskett, 1992: 144). A great deal of the more recent research on leadership has been concerned with the explanation of leadership as an exchange of rewards; as the result of contingency between factors including relationship with subordinates, the setting and the task; as a degree of consensus between the followers' understanding of the leaders' goals and their own needs; as the negotiation of order and meaning with others. All these perspectives demonstrate a shift away from the earlier preoccupation with traits believed to be shared by leaders and towards a more open understanding of the leader in context and in relation to others. But they still perceive the leader as central. Leadership theory paralleled management theory in broadening the nest of contingencies in which the leader/ manager operated, while continuing to regard him or her as central, rational and dominant if not heroic; 'modern-day systems or contingency theory still conveyed the image of managerial work as a social practice characterised by rational planning and control unencumbered by ideological prejudice or material vested interest' (Reed, 1989: 74). A reaction against 'official theory' developed that grew to a tradition of 'real management theory' (Anthony, 1986: 177–9) grounded in empirical obser-vation, which, *inter alia*, emphasized the political behaviour of managers and 'documented the alliances that managers have to form with other individuals and interest groups, within and without their employing organizations, in order to negotiate a viable route between the conflicting pressures and correspond-ing uncertainties that are the very stuff of organizational life' (Reed, 1989: 76). Evidence for this view of leadership comes from studies of the role of general managers – heads of large organizations who can be presumed to exercise the functions of leadership – who operate consistently across the borders of the organization. Stewart (1985) distinguishes managerial patterns of communication including an important category maintained outside the manager's organization. Kotter's (1982) study of general managers stresses the importance of the maintenance of social networks including those that cross the boundaries of departments and the organization itself.

While it is not the prime purpose of this tradition to emphasize that leaders occupy a boundary position in their organizations, that view appears to be perfectly consistent with it and indeed seems to be implied by it. It becomes reasonable to see the leader, in contrast to the romantic account, as patrolling and frequently crossing the frontiers of the organization. This alternative percep-tion of leadership is also entailed by the common conception of the leader as representative of the corporation or community: where else – apart from factions within – is representation made but in the outside world?

One of the necessary functions of leadership, as real theory demonstrates, is the negotiation of order and meaning with others who are outside internal control. Alternatively, an import-ant activity of the leader is to keep the organization in touch with reality as it is perceived by others. The danger in the neo-romantic explanation of leadership is that it overrides this relationship; it contributes to the Nietzschean conception of the isolated hero, remote from the influence of the world lest he should come to terms with, rather than conquer, it. The current emphasis on the heroic influence of the leader on culture is likely to exaggerate a weakness to which leaders are already suscep-tible.

Everyone knows that all power corrupts. Part of the apparatus of financial and bureaucratic control is directed upwards at limiting this tendency. Recent financial scandals such as the Guinness affair and the mystery of the Maxwell employees' pension fund demonstrate both the necessity and the inadequacy of legal and organizational controls. Leaders, just like the rest of us, cannot always be trusted not to act in their own interest at the expense of that of the organization. Recent enquiries into the Maxwell companies suggest that Sir Robert was the 'victim of deception' as well as its perpetrator and that the deception was carried out by some of his own managers: 'a number of senior managers of Panini, his Italian-based football sticker company were for years running a rival operation. While they reported to Maxwell and senior executives at Maxwell Communications Corporation, they also set up and managed Stickline, Panini's closest rival' (*The Independent on Sunday*, Business, 31 May 1992). So successful were their clandestine operations that Panini was placed under administration and seemed likely to be sold for half of what Maxwell paid for it. Readers of Robert Jackall's *Moral Mazes* (1988) will not be surprised by such a story. It simply illustrates his conclusion that some of the CEOs that he studied were motivated entirely by self-aggrandisement with total disregard for the interest of their corporations. Exceptions, no doubt, but they demonstrate the danger in leadership, particularly when it is accompanied by charismatic quality, consummate acting ability and a tendency for immediate subordinates to agree.

Leaders can be very dangerous people. A natural leader can be a disastrous influence on events, as the comrades of Colonel Custer might have testified had they lived. The qualities of leadership do not necessarily define good management, in some circumstances they can negate it, to the acclaim of those who are led.

They are also likely to distance themselves, in some circumstances, from those who are led whether they are acclaimed or not. Kipnis (1976) argues, on the basis of laboratory experiments, that the stronger the influence over others that holders of power believe they possess, the more contemptuous toward those influenced by them they become and the more likely they are to maintain distance from them and to prefer still more coercive means of influence. Smith and Peterson (1988) argue that this tendency may be countered by other power holders who may qualify immoderate behaviour in subordinate managers in the interest of good will or morale. But there is other evidence for the existence of a tendency for the powerful to become separated from others. In an account of experiments on communication structures, Mulder (1966) reported that

> there appears to be a tendency, on the one hand towards reducing distance between oneself and the more powerful, provided that the distance is not initially too great; and, on the other hand, to creating distance between oneself and the less powerful, provided that the distance is not initially too small'. (p. 27)

But if the distance between the individual and the powerful is too great, the individual will not pursue power: 'in such cases, the energy may be directed into other directions, for instance solidarity with other powerless group members' (p. 261).

Any psychological explanation of the distance between the powerful and the powerless is likely to be exaggerated by processes of cultural control. Power gives leaders the satisfactions of membership and its concomitant, the exclusion of others. It is inevitable and necessary that leaders identify themselves with 'their' organization and, in the process, that they define it in terms of what it excludes, its competitors, trade unions or government agencies of control. Part of the function of leadership, it has been suggested, is in the definition and management of boundaries. It may also be inevitable that leaders are subject to some confusion about where the lines are to be drawn. The inadequacy and weakness of the individual is transformed by the processes of corporate culture into the powerful and transcendent community (Hopfl, 1991). The manufacture and promulgation of corporate culture, whatever its effects on those excluded from power to control it, reinforces the leader's identity with corporate activity and gives it meaning that transcends the self. Any evidence that the boundary lines of the corporation actually exclude employees of the organization is likely to be unwelcome and to be suppressed because it will damage the leaders' perception of their power and those less powerful that cluster around them. It will be deemed, in other words, to diminish the ability of leaders to provide corporate meaning for themselves and others.

Corporate culture, while a necessary comfort for leaders, can dangerously enlarge the distance between leaders and led while concealing the existence of the danger from the leaders. Even Schein asserts that while 'our analysis of leadership to this point has tacitly assumed that while subordinates and others may interpret events somewhat differently, they do concede that the leader has the right to manage the meaning of events' (Schein, 1985: 2). Do they? We know of the existence of sub-cultures in occupational communities and profession, some of them qualifying to be described as 'strong' cultures in their own right and some of them concerned to provide the comparatively powerless with a meaning of events alternative to that provided by the leadership. The leaders' definition of the corporate culture is assumed to extend to the boundaries of the organization that they lead and that it will provide a meaning for the lives of subordinates acceptable to them, 'but from the perspective of these groups, colonies within the empire, the right to manage the meaning of events, the imperial culture, may seem like the sophisticated disguise of economic power' (Anthony, 1990: 5).

The contest between the meaning of events contributed by leaders and the meanings emerging from strong sub-cultures may be difficult to judge in terms of which contributes most to organizational survival. In the contest between managerial values and leadership in the NHS, it may yet turn out to be the professional culture that more closely enshrines not only the health of the patient but the health of the organization. From this alternative perspective, it may be management and leadership that appears as a sub-culture, endowed with dangerous abilities to protect them from critical inspection (Gowler and Legge, 1986). There are other circumstances, revealed to us in recent revelations of the affairs of BICC, Maxwell Enterprises, Guinness, Barlow Clowes, where the corporate culture of the leadership is more obviously contrary to the interest of all except the leaders. In such conditions, the threat to corporate good is more likely to come from corporate culture represented by corporate leadership.

These, no doubt exceptional, circumstances remind us that the influence of leaders on culture can be very bad for the led. They also remind us of the inherently dangerous nature of the power of cultural enclosure and the explanation for its advocacy in the cultural management literature: that it lies beyond explication and perilously near protection from the ability of reason to criticize it. Leaders too, for quite different reasons, are often protected from criticism. The combination of cultural leadership can be a powerful defence against the world. Confronted with the near-magical power to manage meaning, we need to approach corporate culture with great caution. We need to attempt to submit its construction and implementation to social and moral criticism, an endeavour notably lacking in management theorizing and believed to be beyond the concern of managers.

If all this were out of a concern for the well-being of those who are the subject of cultural control, that concern might well be exaggerated: subordinates and communities have their own cultural defences. It is their existence that explains the drive to enclose them and it is the naivety of the attempt that may provide reassurance. The real concern may be for the leaders and what may become of them and for their effect on their organizations' performance.

To the extent that corporate culture can be seen as a sub-culture, it represents the values and beliefs of senior managers, leaders, projected however unrealistically, on to the organization as a whole. As a sub-culture, it encloses its occupants in meaning and expectations and excludes those who recognize its boundaries and who see that the way they do things there are not the ways that are familiar to outsiders. The peculiarity of the sub-culture of corporate leadership, is that it is imperial, its values are believed to be widely shared by its subjects, despite the continuing necessity for coercive controls. Reports to the effect that corporate values are not matters of general conviction are tantamount to the acknowledgement of disloyalty and disaffection and evidence of inept and ineffective leadership. In any case, it is in the nature of missionaries to be evangelical and to incorporate in their own belief system the certainty that truth must be acceptable to all, and we know that leaders are missionaries because this is what they and their consultants tell us. Belief in the necessary loyalty of subordinates and a spiritual concern for their salvation combine to filter out evidence contrary to the enclosure of corporate culture. The values of the leader, predisposed to find evidence of general support, are systematically reinforced by the hierarchical apparatus of control that suppresses disagreement and interprets 'resigned behavioural compliance' as wholehearted conviction. In this respect, leaders are easily led, enclosed by their own constructions against the world and secured against intrusion by values designed to prevent damage. The cultural apparatus aimed at the control of others begins to be threatened, not by others, but by its own certitude. Because it incorporates self-validating techniques designed for the comfort and security of those it encloses, the techniques function so successfully that there can be no intrusion and no correction of error. The narratives of leadership and legendary heroism convince ordinary mortals of the fiction – in a world in which the fictional re-writing of history is recommended as preferable to the truth – of infallibility. Already dangerously prone to misconception about the reliability of their own values, leaders are stimulated to further confidence by the advice that they should abandon the mere management of their organizations because 'one of the most decisive functions of leadership may well be the creation, the management and – if and when they become necessary – the destruction of culture' (Schein, 1985: 9).

Yet it is obvious that leaders can and do contribute significantly to effective performance and significant change. An excellent account of how they do this is to be found in chapter 8 of Kotter and Heskett's (1992) *Corporate Culture and Performance*. They do it by openness to information and dialogue, by clear direction, by motivation and example. And they seem to succeed by influencing the norms of group behaviour rather than by seeking to implant new and grandiose statements of corporate culture. That course, in isolation from other more practical change, is likely to lead only to the isolation of the leaders.

8

CULTURE VERSUS REASON

'The battle-lines are now clear: it is individual reason versus collective culture' (Gellner, 1992: 8). Thus Gellner describes the divide between the Cartesian conviction that reason alone can establish truth and reliability and the influence of a collective past handed down to us through the medium of culture. What Descartes proposed, says Gellner, 'is a programme for man's liberation from culture' (p. 13).

It comes as a shock to be reminded that culture can be seen as the enemy of reason. We have come to associate culture with understanding, itself part of the process of rational discovery of the way societies, as well as organizations, work and we have gone on to apply this rational understanding so as to try to subordinate culture to the organization's pursuit of economic goals. This is an entirely rational process in which culture and reason are intimately associated. To be reminded that they are at odds is surprising. This is because of a convergence, as Williams et al. (1989) called it, between two approaches, the idealist and the materialist. The former is concerned with the spirit of a society represented in its language, art and ways of thinking. The latter concerns itself with a study of the observable laws of social organizations and particularly of institutions, often conducted along lines similar to those of the natural sciences. Williams comments that the two traditions had little to say to each other. To the extent that communication developed between the two, we have reached or are exploring a relationship between the material, 'objective' laws and the historical cultural 'spirit' that influenced them. In that case the exploration of culture is enriched but continues to see itself as a rational enquiry. To the extent that it remains concerned with material laws exclusively, it encourages the conviction that they are controllable. In either case, culture is seen as friendly, amenable to the rational processes by which it is studied and, above all, contributing to control.

The study of management organizations is caught up with culture as a means of enhancing control rather than understanding. All the potent carriers of meaning: myth, legend, narrative, ritual and symbol, are presented and welcomed as additional tools in management's equipment but deemed to be so powerful that they may yet serve to make the others redundant. Culture becomes an extension of science but an extension that does not depart from its offer of rationality and predictability. It is science, or what it offers, by other means and without the painstaking work.

It is hardly surprising, then, given the explanation for its promotion, that culture and its accoutrements were seen as benign and promising. There is, however, one indication that has been present throughout this discussion of cultural management, of a persistent distinction between the material and the cultural, and that is in the suspicion with which the one continues to regard the other. Culture, it is claimed along with the other soft-system strategies, can supplement or even replace the specious claims of science to provide the principles of management. So, we have seen numerous examples of the suspicion with which rational systems are regarded and criticisms of the negative consequences of bureaucratic methods of control. These rest upon the assertion that scientific methods of analysis and control cannot be applied to human beings or to organizations operated by them without losing their human capacities or actively antagonizing them. The two traditions still find it difficult to communicate with each other, each seems to see itself as self-sufficient, the one establishing systems without people, the other cultures without systems. What they have in common is the claimed capacity to exercise control. Paradoxically, it is the social sciences' recognition of the irrational that enhances its claim to control the most effectively. Much of the cultural paraphernalia recommended in the literature of cultural management is presented in terms of a power to influence which is beyond the dilution of rational criticism and debate. Cultural constructions, backed by the impenetrable influence of ideology, can resolve contradictions that present themselves merely at the level of rational consciousness. The influence of metaphor lies in its duality of meaning, its ability to associate like with unlike. The significance of symbols is that they are signs that elicit meanings that do not relate to them. Legends are stories of the past that are irrefutable and can, therefore, securely serve as guides to present action. Myths are universal explanations that are meaningful because they are untestable. All in all, culture seems to offer the service of dark forces for managerial purpose.

Before we all came to be enthralled, like our unsophisticated, pre-scientific ancestors, by the reintroduction of these old terms in new texts, we might remember that they were often attributed rather more doubtful meanings in our common speech. We would often talk of myths as dangerous and untrue; to call something 'a myth' would be to dismiss it. Symbols might be seen to have doubtful value; 'merely' symbolic. Metaphors might be revealed in argument before their consequential dismissal from consideration. Legends were for the attention of children before they went on to study history. The double meaning of so many cultural terms continues to be significant, indeed it is the scientific study of culture that has revealed its significance. It suggests that culture is itself a doppleganger, reflecting our existence in another world.

If that is so, the determination to use the cultural apparatus for the purpose of the deliberate manipulation of meaning is likely to be an uncertain business. Cultural terms are powerful because of their ambiguity and that implies that meaning may be very difficult to control. Even the words in the mission statements are doubtful. 'Participation' can mean anything from a polite enquiry about preference for the colour of the staffroom walls to the most full-blooded experiment in syndicalist workers control (the former is often represented by works councils, the latter by workers' councils). Team building can be an open or a dictatorial process and the term may be used to disguise the one in order to present it as the other. In some circumstances 'hierarchies become obfuscated by the use of a form of "we" language which made no division between senior management and clerical temp' with continual references to 'our' goals and 'our' company (Kerfoot and Knights, 1992). Obfuscation may be the intention, but if subordinate perceptions of the reality of hierarchies and the real ownership of goals remain unchanged, the new words may clarify rather than obscure the real meanings imputed to the terms and the real differences in interest that they signify.

The choice of words and language receives a great deal of attention in discussion of the management of culture, some of it critical, meant to unmask the hidden intentions of the managers. In one such critical unmasking, 'discourse technology' is defined as 'types of discourse which involve the more or less self-conscious application of social scientific knowledge for purposes of bureaucratic control' (Fairclough, 1989: 211). The criticism seems to be confined to the more or less innocent aspirations of bureaucratic control, comparatively easy to penetrate and relatively ineffective in results. It is the perception of that ineffectiveness that has moved social science on to the new frontier of culture. Bureaucratic control, from the perspective of the controllers, unfortunately leaves subordinates free, partly because they possess their own cultural defences. So the defences must be broken.

The same mechanistic paradigm is at work here, subjecting culture to the same assumption that what is understood in terms of analysis and categorization can be controlled, further, that the only purpose of understanding is to achieve control because that is the function of science. But the ambitions for cultural control are as likely to be thwarted as were the intentions of bureaucracy but this time with potentially more dangerous consequences.

The first respect in which culture can continue to be seen as the enemy of reason – if reason is associated with purpose and its systematic realization – lies in its complexity and unpredictability. The proposals to manage culture do not take account of cultural independence from control. If they did, the proposers would be out of business. Cultures are owned by their inhabitants. Cultures have to provide explanations and means for the survival of communities and those facilities are compounds of cooperation and necessary defences against the powerful, including their leaders. It is in the nature of cultures to be influenced by leaders, to be moulded by the structures of authority, but also to be capable of providing space within the moulds. Some part of the character of cultures is that they are defensive, hence the boundaries that demarcate them and that we commonly observe. Members of sub-cultures do not always accept – they may even bitterly reject – the cultural accounts given of them by outsiders, including their leaders. The legends of Dunkirk or Ypres, as they were told at the time, are not the same as the stories told by the survivors (the distinctive sub-culture of the British Army: sardonic, derisory and comically unheroic, is beautifully demonstrated in Brophy and Partridge, 1969). The first danger to the intention of greater organizational control is, then, that culture is likely to be uncontrollable or, if you like, unreasonable.

The second danger is to the organization or, as we saw in the last section, to its leadership, not simply in terms of its propensity to become lost but rather because of the kind of culture it is prone to promote more particularly when it is lost. The assumption that the interests of others are entirely the same as one's own is usually revealed by experience to be naive: if not it becomes dangerous. The assumption that meanings are the same and, if not, that they can be made to be the same, flows from the former error and leads to even more dangerous consequences.

The pursuit of one culture in substitution for the muddled complexity of sub-cultures and cultural segmentation is most familiar and visible in the political sphere. Here it has been pursued in an attempt to impose theocratic rule as in Calvin's Geneva of the sixteenth century, or in order to command adherence through conviction to a political system of belief. Among the best known examples of the latter in the twentieth century, so far, have been the Soviet Union and Nazi Germany. Among the characteristics of both these regimes were:

- An unshakeable conviction on the part of the leadership that their ultimate purpose was good and right.

93

- The consequential belief that any method was justified in the pursuit of that purpose – that the end justifies the means – followed by the use of institutions of terror and extermination.
- The inability to accept criticism, opposition or access to any alternative political or moral standpoint, either to the overall purpose or to the instrumental means of achieving it.

One of the best accounts of both the philosophical weaknesses and the awful results of such closed ideologies is to be found in Karl Popper's (1945) *The Open Society and its Enemies*. A more vivid, fictional treatment is familiar in George Orwell's *1984* in which the author extends the range of available totalitarian controls to include the manipulation of language, meaning and history. Examples of the recommendation of an argued necessity for cultural control are not confined to the notoriously bestial. The much more benign, well-intentioned and widely accepted – at least in enlightened circles – case for ecological protection by enforced 'politics of frugality' has been criticized for its mixture of certitude and concealment (Anthony, 1977).

The point of this excursion into the more alarming areas of political extremism is not, it must be emphasized, in order to draw any parallel between the methods and intentions of Stalin or Hitler and those of corporate managers. It is to suggest that the utilization of cultural control, whether it be in states or business enterprises, is likely to be attended by the same incipient dangers. Cultural management, if it is pursued out of conviction, is likely to perceive opposition as threatening and therefore to exclude it from consideration. In so far as its ambition is a state of cultural unity – albeit, merely in the successful marketing of doughnuts (Deal and Kennedy, 1982) – it is incapable of recognizing the legitimacy of criticism, either moral or practical. The control of a culture of doughnut production is a lot safer and leaves us all sleeping easier than the control of the culture of a state, but they each threaten the application of forces that are admired because they are unreasonable: they are, both, dark rather than illuminating and both are photophobic, prone to avoid the light.

In this general sense, culture can still be represented as the enemy of reason; irrational in its content, in the purpose for which its control is sought and in its defences against intrusion and criticism. It is also likely to produce results opposite to those that it pursues. Openness, empowerment, risk-taking and responsibility – all avowed objectives in corporate cultural management – are likely to be suppressed by subordination to cultural authority by the methods it imposes and to be less open to individuality than the bureaucracies that are to be supplanted.

Cultural control is almost by definition likely to misunderstand the true complexity and variety of culture, the raw material upon which it works. Here, finally, is a cause for optimism. It is reinforced in those grandiose examples of attempted cultural control, Nazi Germany and the Soviet Union. Two of the most powerful states in the world devoted resources, education, surveillance, propaganda of advanced sophistication and every known means of socialization, backed at least in the one case by an entrenched ideology widely admired in parts of the West for its commanding authority, to reveal, after their collapse, continuing scepticism. Worse, in the case of the Soviet Union, the unplanned and endemic system of economic corruption was sufficiently vigorous not only to have survived but apparently to provide the only viable system alternative to the collapse of the state machine. Against such an example of failure, what price the culture of doughnuts?

9

CULTURE IN
PERSPECTIVE

The objection to the more superficial attempts to manage culture or to substitute for it quickly manufactured corporate cultures, is that they rest upon a misunderstanding of the nature of culture, its strength, complexity and influence upon organizational behaviour. The objection should not be understood as a rejection of the importance of culture itself or of its significance to managers.

Cultures – of communities or organizations, the relationship between the two will have to be explored shortly – are real. An objection to Gareth Morgan's (1986) inclusion of culture among the metaphors of organization is that organizations are not merely 'like' cultures, they *are* cultures. Culture encloses us in a web of shared meanings, understandings, obligations and expectations and without that enclosure we would find it impossible to survive in any communal relationship and, therefore, impossible to survive at all. But cultures do not entirely determine our behaviour for two reasons: cultures that persist are dynamic, they adapt to changes in their environments and in social structures and are open to our influence (to the influence of some of us more than others); cultures are also segmented both spatially and temporally (Turner, 1971), we are members of more than one at a time, they overlap and each influences and is influenced by the others. The significance of culture is well attested in a tradition of study in one of the most authoritative of the social sciences; anthropology. There is little room for doubt about the reality of cultural influence.

It is the reliability of the evidence that appears to attract the attention of management, evidence of a new source of power available for the exercise of more effective control. The evidence seems even to offer the prospect of total control, not merely of behaviour but of meaning itself; culture is seen as a latent source of power, available to meet the constant demand for managerial control over subordinates – and managers. The meeting between the two, the supply and the demand, takes place in the consultancy market and the result is the development of corporate cultural management. That development is proper and inevitable, the product of increasing sophistication in the understanding of organizational behaviour and the influences upon it. Indeed it is the apparent promise of the potency of cultural influence that has generated 'the greatest anticipation, excitement and debate' in the field of organizational behaviour (Wilson and Rosenfeld, 1990: 234). It has also attracted the attention of chief executives advised by consultants that culture alone and at last can provide total commitment and absolute cooperation in the whole-hearted pursuit of corporate goals, as they are defined by the chief executive.

At this point there emerges, not an extension of the accumulated understanding – some of it, as in any field of enquiry, contested – achieved in the various social sciences, but the opposite. The psychological evidence of differences in personal goals and aptitudes and of differences in personality, the various effects of the influences of nurture and of group influences; the sociological understanding of differences of interest, of class formation, socialization and structuration; the anthropologist's accounts of social and cultural complexity, all are overturned in the happy expectation of simple recipes for reaching unified purpose and understanding and their substitution for the irksome complexity of reality. The current recipe is that a corporate culture can be created and imposed on a variety of individuals and groups, irrespective of their different interests, backgrounds, perspectives and different degrees of access to power.

nconvincing prospectus by which cultural management
~~been~~ promoted is given a specious attractiveness by some of
the special offers that it includes. The instruments of change
seem to be daringly new and conveniently protected from
inspection. As the old familiar routines of control inevitably failed
to deliver what was hoped for them, they have yielded to the
mysterious promise of the legendary, the mythical and the
symbolic. But it is a forgivable misunderstanding that seeks to
translate the latent influence of culture into harnessed energy.

The misunderstanding rests upon the failure to acknowledge
several qualifications attending the influence of culture on
change. The first is that culture cannot be treated simply as a
resource, to be separately managed. Culture represents a series
of relationships rather than a commodity. While it is surprising
that a concept so vague and vaporous has commanded managerial attention, it is understandable that any effort to apply it has
gone astray. The attempt has diverted attention from the reality
of culture and its true significance in the management of
organizations and change.

Structure

Culture is such a cloudy concept that it is easy to lose sight of this
reality and to risk encouraging myopia rather than clear-
sightedness by more and more vaporous attempts to describe it.
To avoid that risk it must be stressed that culture emerges from
history, is rooted in practice, sustained by structures and
becomes habitual – and therefore unconscious and unthinking –
as the result of routines of repeated behaviour. The relationship
between culture and structure is so close that many accounts of
culture and how to change it merge imperceptibly into descriptions of structure; as Lee and Lawrence (1985) put it, 'the first
possibility is that one views structure as a part determinant of
culture . . . the second . . . is that structural items are actually
viewed as part of the culture' (p. 115). It is a matter of no great
moment which view prevails except that the confusion reminds
us that the means recommended for cultural change often take
structural form. What we should remember is that organizational

cultures are indissolubly linked with structure, inter-dependent and reflective. The means to change culture must be accompanied by structural change, otherwise the 'new' culture will be contradicted by the old structures and their concrete as well as symbolic reminders that nothing real has changed and that the core values of the organization continue to be demonstrated by 'the way we do things here', no matter what we say. Structures and the actual performance and behaviour that they require, permit and proscribe, are statements of values in action and, if they are standing contradictions of the espoused values of the organization's management, the result is likely to be cynicism and personal or organizational breakdown. Structures are not the sole determinants of cultural formation but they are most potent influences upon it. They also have the singular advantage, in the miasmas of the cultural milieu, of visibility; they can be observed – and changed – by planned action and they are equally visible to inhabitants as clear signals of what, in practice, really matters to those who direct the organization's affairs.

The clarity of these structural signals can be an embarrassment to management and, paradoxically, an explanation of the preference current in some quarters for managing culture rather than managing the organization. A preoccupation with cultural management can be a sign of managerial confusion about what to do and how to change: it becomes much easier to produce visions than strategies.

On the other hand, accounts of significant and successful change programmes that have been undertaken at Cadbury (Smith et al., 1990) or at ICI (Pettigrew, 1985), relate cultural change to strategic, structural and political processes. They also demonstrate that success is often accompanied by difficulty and conflict. Those painful accompaniments may not be the means by which intended change is brought about, but their deliberate avoidance by the simple expedient of an announcement that the organization's values have changed, or that they will change as from Monday next, is most unlikely to succeed.

Once again, this is not to suggest that cultural change is unimportant or that it cannot be managed. The exposition of the values that are held to be important, the influence of leaders, of role modelling, example and reward are important ingredients in change, but they are ingredients that must be consistent with reality and purpose. In an admirable discussion of the relationship between culture and practice and structure, Kotter and Heskett (1992) conclude:

> our studies clearly show that certain kinds of corporate culture help, while others undermine, long-term economic performance [and that] strong cultures with practices that do not fit a company's context can actually lead intelligent people to behave in ways that are destructive – that systematically undermine an organization's ability to survive and prosper. (pp. 141–2).

Technology

Structural influence upon culture is closely related to technology. A great deal of the explanation of the character of industrial sectors has been explained in terms of the dominating influence of the prevailing technology of manufacture. The marked occupational culture of the coal mining industry has been largely attributed to the confined setting, the strong formation of group membership, physical hardship and danger, and social and geographical isolation, all consequent upon the nature of mining. More specific associations with changes in the technology of mining were argued in studies by Trist and Bamforth (1951), when the culture of closely bonded groups in pillar and stall mining was described as having been destroyed – with damaging consequences – in the introduction of long-wall techniques of coal extraction. There is a suggestion in the work that management's choice of production methods should be influenced by the social patterns of cooperation which they are believed to provide. This argument for technological choice is open to two objections: it ignores the unpredictable reactions and patterns of behaviour of employees and groups; and managerial choice is strictly limited by technological determinism, governed by considerations of labour cost, productivity and profit. There is little doubt that it is these considerations rather than any concern with social and cultural planning that have influenced developments in mining and other industries.

The contemporary interest in the influence of technology on culture has shifted from the old to new technologies. The introduction of computer controlled materials requirements planning and manufacturing resources planning may encourage individualism, flexibility and delegation (Kinnie, 1989) and, in turn, contribute to changing the culture of the enterprise. On a wider scale, the vast increase in the availability of information and computerized display and presentation is likely to change the view that the organization takes of itself, that is of its cultural construction. In one particular respect, computerized information systems – the 'information panopticon' as Zuboff (1988) calls it – extends the potential for total surveillance of the organization's inhabitants including its managers. The outcome and the cultural consequences of this extension remain in doubt, however. There is a division between a nightmare prediction of omniscient control asserting total compliance and an alternative in which new and unpredictable spaces are opened up by skilful operators with the ability to use new techniques and power to their own advantage.

How the balance between these contradictory consequences will be worked through, and what its longer-term impact on organizational design will be, are matters which will be primarily determined by the strategic choices emerging from the power struggles engaged in by conflicting social, political and economic interests. (Reed, 1992: 275)

Technology, in all its forms, is a potent influence on organizational design and tasks and therefore on organizational culture. The potential exists for harnessing technology to the deliberate shaping of culture. In practice, the relationship is not always sought; there is little articulation, for example, between technological planning and HRM (Kinnie, 1989; Storey and Sisson, 1989). But perhaps it is the formidable disagreement about the cultural consequences of technological change that reminds us of the difficulty of cultural prediction and planning, of the extraordinary problems in the way of engaging in the management of culture, even in the area of the acknowledged and indisputable influence of technology.

Leaders

Leaders, as the most visible representatives and the most powerful individual moulders of values in action, exercise a significant influence on cultural formation and change. But we have seen that their influence can be exaggerated and, in some cases, be dangerous, even baleful. Once again, it is the pursuit of easy paths to comprehensive change, associated with the belief that complex organizations are command structures in which every one does what they are told and, even more singular, that every one believes what they are told. Put in those terms, the straightforward association between culture and leadership – 'they are two sides of the same coin' – appears as another deceptively simple solution to the complex problem of change and control. The leader becomes the opposite of the sacrificial goat that carries all sin, the leader is the visionary who has talked with God and who descends the mountain carrying the law.

Such rare events are reported to have occurred, of course. Leaders have converted whole peoples to a faith, led nations to conquest, required and obtained great sacrifices and, in the process, transformed by their example entire cultures. These circumstances are usually attended by the simplicity and sometimes the grand nobility of the transformational appeal; nothing has to be done except to follow. Sadler cites the leadership by General Slim of the British 14th Army in Burma during the Second World War as 'an outstanding example of the achievement of cultural change' (Sadler, 1988: 129). But, apart from the imaginative means he used, General Slim, had the advantage of a singularly simple purpose, to destroy the enemy (as a matter of fact, in the overall context of the cultural movement it had, perhaps, greater significance; 'to destroy the Japanese army'). It is for this reason, perhaps, that the majority of leadership researchers are described as being 'wedded to the fundamental tenets of rational model ideas' of organizations and their pursuit of clearly determined goals (Bryman, 1986: 174). But the comparative simplicity of goal directed behaviour has been subjected to criticism from explanations of leadership and management as are concerned in political relationships and struggles directed at more narrowly defined, sectional and even personal goals. And if

a great deal of leadership is not concerned with broad organizational goals 'but has a more personal focus, then it is small
wonder that the correlations between leadership style and
performance are so often small and inconsistent' (p. 176).

The relationship between leadership and organizational performance may well be tenuous, but that does not necessarily
remove the influence of the leader on organizational culture. The
influence is asserted in three ways: on the leader's determination
of structure, of the extent and speed of technological change –
subjects already discussed but themselves related to leader
decision-making and not, therefore, independent variables – and
the leader's formulation of other people's reality.

This is the area in which leadership is seen to possess
transformational possibilities. The ability of the leader to re-
formulate the understanding of others seems to depend upon
two characteristic features; symbolic reconstruction and deliberate motivation. Symbolic reconstruction is a 'natural' process in
which the way we see things is in part the result of the way they
are told and communicated to us. Leaders necessarily achieve a
degree of generalization in their accounts and stories of the
organization; several forces including their own necessary ignor-
ance, conspire to avoid detail and confusing complexity in the
presentation of the broad picture. General descriptions tend to
rely on the utility of metaphor – the linkage of similarities – and
the rapid connections of the dissimilar achieved by symbolism;
they are both necessary instruments of generalization. But they
also share the capacity to affect emotional response and to
construct emotional meaning. The language of leaders is thus
predisposed to useful concision and to the possibility of
emotional manipulation. Formless events are shaped into meaningful accounts and the meanings may be deliberately shaped by
leadership. The humiliation of the British defeat in France is
transformed into the legend of Dunkirk. The Challenger disaster
in the USA is turned by the President's address to the nation into
an occasion for solidarity and even glory: the victims are
compared to Drake, they 'slipped the surly bonds of earth to
touch the face of God'. Sir Michael Edwardes not only changes
the structure of British Leyland, he reconstructs by his language
its meaning (Edwardes, 1983).

The account of the transformation of British Airways under the leadership of Lord King and Sir Colin Marshall has a lot to say about transformational leadership, but it insists that the impact of leadership cannot be directed at values unsupported by practice, that there has to be 'internal consistency' (Hampden-Turner, 1990). The consistency must be between created meanings and the reality of the organization as it is experienced by employees and, in this case, customers. There are limits, in short, on the magical powers attributed to leaders, but within those limits they have considerable power to create not only the image of the organization but its meaning.

Cultures can be changed and, therefore, managed, but the process must take into account the more material features of the organization as well as the representations that are made of it. Meaning is not entirely a matter of representation; for most of us representation must have some relationship to the reality of our experience. Leaders can influence organizational culture, but their attempt to substitute for it an unreal conception of corporate culture, which often turns out to be a generalization of their own personal perspective transposed upon the whole, is likely to be a misconception. In Chapter 5 we looked at the dangers to management in that attempt and in Chapter 6 at the dangerous defence capabilities of leaders that can protect them from reality and encourage them to maintain their effort in the mistaken belief that it has succeeded.

One of the realities that must be taken into account in the management of culture is the values and beliefs of those to be submitted to its influence and control. It is a measure of the ideological consensus underlying the discussion of cultural management that, while the significance of management values are taken for granted, the culture of subordinates is seen as an empty space, to be worked upon at will. The only matter for debate in the literature is how it can best be done, not about the comparative values of the subordinate and their comparative worth. While the whole conception of cultural management rests upon the possibility of choice on the part of management, choice is not conceived of as available to 'lower participants' who are, willy-nilly, to be brought to participate in the corporate culture. But there *is* choice.

In contrast to participation in a culture of birth, participation in an organizational culture is more temporary or transitory and more a matter of voluntary choice (though not necessarily the product of a conscious rational decision process). In the former, the core culture of shared values, 'culture can be extremely difficult to change' (Kotter and Heskett, 1992: 4). In the latter, the culture of norms of behaviour, change is easier to bring about, but it may be sufficient for the organization's purpose. Ultimately, one is a participant in a particular culture 'to the extent that one considers him or herself to be a member' (Louis, 1983: 49).

Choice may be made in terms of comparisons with a culture of birth and its heritage of core values, or with the individual's experience of the reality of life in the organization. Choice may also be a matter of taste or, more precisely, the result of an assessment of the moral character of the culture on offer.

Cultural comparisons

Some attention has been paid to international cultural comparisons, particularly in the work of Hofstede (1980) who concluded, *inter alia*, on the basis of international data that American managers were likely to value individuality and striving for success higher than other societies. But there seems to be little managerial attention to comparative cultural characteristics in different levels and compartments of the organization, indeed, such an interest is almost precluded by the paradigm assumptions of unity from which cultural management sets forth. This may represent another unreality which cultural management needs to correct before it becomes a more practical endeavour.

It is evident that large organizations are composed of nested and inter-acting sub-cultures, divided both laterally and vertically. The management of corporate culture is, in part, a process of presenting one of them as coextensive with the whole and of recruiting the others to accept that presentation. It is not so evident that the success of the effort rests to some extent on the choice exercised by the recruits. The degree to which we are

105

prepared to see ourselves as members of a culture which is only partial in its enclosure – that is, in cultures based on work – may well depend on our assessment of its moral character.

The relevance of moral issues to economic organizations is not immediately apparent. The relevance of moral characteristics to cultures is direct and unarguable. Communities are held together by reciprocal relationships of obligation and responsibility which do not have to be constantly specified or re-negotiated, by norms of reciprocity as Gouldner calls them (for a discussion of this characteristic and its demonstration in the work of Redfield, in Gouldner and in Fox, see Anthony, 1986: chs 3 and 7). Communities are developed upon economic and geographical foundations but they are sustained by moral relationships and expectations. To the extent that economic organizations are communities they too are bound by moral relationships, although, like the organizational community itself, they may be weaker and more ephemeral. In so far as the power of management needs to seek legitimate authority over its subordinates, that authority must be established on moral grounds. To the extent that organizations wish to turn themselves into or to present themselves as communities, they have to find a moral basis for the presentation. Since it is the purpose of the management of corporate culture to assert that the organization is a community composed of cooperating members bound by the same purpose and values, the reality of its claim must be subject to moral inspection. If, as the result of that inspection, we are not impressed by the moral character of the purported community we will not see ourselves obligated to its expectations or enclosed by its membership. We will stay outside, although purely self-interested economic considerations will, no doubt, require some acting ability on our part.

Such talk of the moral features of organizations may seem strange in terms of the economic perspectives from which they are usually explained, but it is the organizations and their leaders who are leading themselves into this critique. The discussion will also seem strange from the post-modernist standpoint which asserts that the image of the organization is the thing itself, the product, with which, because we live in a world of images, no comparison with the 'real' is possible. If knowledge and the whole accumulated apparatus of empirical enquiry is dismissed as subject to ideological influence, sectional interest and the contested claim that language itself can represent the real, then 'a genuine interest in discovering the nature of things in themselves seems both naive and misleading' (Gergen, 1992: 213). And so the attempt to arrive at rational understandings of organization is doomed. Post-modernists, on the other hand would prefer to see themselves 'as balloon craftsmen – setting aloft vehicles for public amusement' (p. 216). Where one goes after that is a problem, as Gergen acknowledges ('it is difficult . . . to generate theories where there is no existing forestructure of intelligibility to be extended and elaborated' (p. 217). It must be said that he does try, but the attempt is lost on this particular reader). If nothing can reliably be said about organizations, there is nothing to say about their cultures and any attempt to compare them with reality is risible.

Oddly enough, the straightforward accounts of cultural management seem to point in the same direction, to argue that both the methods and the results of cultural construction are secure from rational enquiry. If, as Pondy (1983) suggests, the function of metaphor and myth is to 'place explanation beyond doubt and argumentation' (p. 163) then some of that security is likely to rub off on the product they function to create. If the product, culture, is an enclosure in a web of meanings, it is difficult to escape from it in order to submit it to criticism.

But even if everything is for the amusement of the public, something can be said. Jokes are judged by the severest empirical test; whether they make us laugh or not. And if all we have is images, even if we cannot ask what they represent we may criticize them as images, the subject of aesthetic and moral judgement. We have our feelings, even if our capacity to reason is in doubt (that doubt, incidentally, is contemptuously dismissed in the conclusion to Gellner's *Reason and Culture* (1992)). Our capacity to reject images cannot be removed either by their manufacturers or by the manufacturers' critics who, in nihilistic desperation, reject everything for the sake of security.

From our roughly constructed bastion we can say that the cultural images of organization must satisfy *some* criteria. At the very least, would-be participants have a degree of choice as to whether and how far they will accept them. They have an alternative because they are, themselves, not bereft of cultural membership and images of their own. They can and do reject the new cultural images and withdraw to their own cultural under-growth in which they may sustain an effective guerrilla war. This is not a phenomenon confined to the shopfloor subordinate: professional groups are formidable compaigners in defense of their cultural values. In that case, whatever the more material interests are that are being defended, the battle is usually fought out on cultural and moral grounds. Choice and the extent to which it leads to participation or rejection is influenced by moral considerations.

There is room for even more individual and social agency in the critical review of a culture. This is particularly the case in the very peculiar circumstances in which corporate cultures are presented to us. They are not just organizational cultures that we enter on recruitment to the BBC or M and S, when we discover them and begin to adapt to them: corporate cultures are manufactured and often presented to the employees, quite often as alternatives to the organizational cultures of which they are already members. Because of their newness they have to be advertised; a great deal of the whole of this discussion has been about the manufacture and advertisement of new, corporate cultures. We do not grow into them, they are presented for our inspection.

It is possible to consider some of the critical criteria they need to satisfy. We are likely to concern ourselves with two questions:

1 What kind of personal behaviour is the corporate culture likely to require of us, if we accept membership?
2 What kind of influence is the corporate culture likely to have on the broader values of the community in which we live?

The first is a personal question the great importance of which is recognized by the selection criteria which accompanies recruit-ment to organizations like IBM or Toyota; perfectly sensible judgements that individuals should be selected for employment who will find the values of the company congenial to their own.

The second is broader and opens the corporate culture or its image to more general review. Perhaps we would say that it should not be overly oppressive. While we would expect an employer to be 'an imperatively coordinated association' (Dah-rendorf, 1959), that is, that we will spend most of our time doing what it tells us to do, and we might or might not expect it to recognize a trade union, or to consult with or inform us about change, or to be benevolent or autocratic – in other respects we might hope that it would reflect the values of our society. We might hope that it would not require us to commit murder, to tell lies in our personal interest as a matter of course or to subordinate all other values and concerns, including our families to a conception of corporate good. At least, we might say, if it sought to do that out of an understandable and legal concern for the interest of its shareholders and chief executive, the process should be open to criticism because it borders on oppression. It might do all these things, short of commanding murder, without risk of public criticism, but not with our own full-hearted approval. We might be driven to work for it but not to join its community.

The risk run in the construction of corporate cultures is that they go too far in the imposition of values directed at economic and sectional ends as the putative values of a community. Any risk to the wider society in such a process of domination is discounted by the probability that it will not work. The threat of enclosure by corporate cultures – and of their isolation from critical review, aided and abetted though that protection is by post-modernist pessimism – does not have to be countered by insurrection, legal constraint, or industrial action. The defences are suitably camouflaged and include, in the last resort, 'resigned behavioural compliance', acting, sardonic withdrawal and cyni-cism. They are, in short, the explanations rehearsed in Chapters 6 and 7 for the likely failure of corporate culture.

Missions, visions and the need for agnosticism

Managing culture is different and the concern with it is proper and necessary. The case presented here is that the management of culture is an important extension of mangement's role. It represents the extension of managers' understanding of the complex relationships and influences that constitute their field of activity, and the better they understand it the more effective they are likely to be, this understanding of organizational culture being an important part of their development.

Organizational culture also provides a means of change. The only reservations that have been expressed here concern gross exaggerations of the speed and extent of the change that can be achieved and of the dangers of its overly optimistic pursuit. Organizational culture is a reality that influences the values and behaviour of its members. Change in core values is difficult to achieve: change in behaviour is easier; 'the change that may be managed is the manifestly observable behaviours *not* the un-observable deep-seated attitudes of individuals' (Ogbonna, 1992: 82). Ogbonna's study of a major UK supermarket reported that its directors believe that 'creating the appropriate culture is an essential prerequisite to success' but he goes on to describe the various obstacles to its achievement. The change programme incorporates a 'smile campaign' designed to make staff provide genuine smiles for customers. What it produces is behavioural compliance rather than the acceptance of the required values. This result may well be typical; 'the cultural change described in the literature may be at the observable behavioural level. . . . At the very best, many attempts to change culture are only success-ful at the overt behavioural level' (p. 90). Finally, Ogbonna speculates if it matters to managers whether or not the required behaviour is based upon internalized values. It probably does not as long as managers are generating behaviour appropriate to their strategies. If they are, much of the concern with achieving change in corporate values is redundant as well as being expensive, unreliable and dangerous. In that sense, managers might do better to forget corporate culture.

There is another sense in which the management of culture might be becoming redundant. The concern with the perceived weakness of bureaucracy was one of the reasons for turning to corporate cultural control in the first place. There are now signs that the ideal of large corporate identity and control is changing. Mature and turbulent markets are now turning attention to the 'virtual firm', concentrating on core competencies and net-working the rest to independent, satellite suppliers (BBC Radio 4. Analysis, Peter Haynes, 4.3.93). Reebok International produces nothing but designs. If the company has to be reinvented, re-thinking relationships with suppliers and with customers, and if the enterprise is no longer to be seen as enclosed in organizational boundaries, what is to be our conception of the organization? It would seem to be necessarily blurred. If a strong sense of corporate identity becomes incompatible with success, the reasons for manufacturing corporate cultures are negated. Agnosticism towards managing corporate culture may be justified by the market processes that once encouraged it. The new enterprises may be better off without cultures because they become as ossified as the bureaucracies they were meant to replace. In the circumstances they might be wiser to confine their attention to achieving appropriate change in behaviour.

REFERENCES

Anthony, P. D. (1977) *The Ideology of Work*. London, Tavistock.

Anthony, P. D. (1986) *The Foundation of Management*. London, Tavistock.

Anthony, P. D. (1990) The paradox of the management of culture or, 'He who leads is lost', *Personnel Review*, 19(4), 3–8.

Argyris, C. (1964) *Integrating the Individual and the Organization*. New York, John Wiley.

Baritz, L. (1965) *The Servants of Power*. New York, John Wiley.

Bate, P. (1992) The impact of organizational culture on approaches to organizational problem solving. In G. Salaman (ed.), *Human Resource Strategies*. London, Sage.

Baxter, B. (1982) *Alienation and Authenticity: Some Consequences for Organized Work*. London, Tavistock.

Bell, D. (1961) *The End of Ideology*. New York, Collier.

Bell, D. (1973) *The Coming of Post-Industrial Society*. New York, Basic Books.

Blackler, F. and Brown, C. (1980) *Whatever Happened to Shell's New Philosophy of Management?* London, Saxon House.

Blauner, R. (1964) *Alienation and Freedom*. Chicago, Chicago University Press.

Brophy, J. and Partridge, E. (1969) *The Long Trail*. London, Sphere.

Bryman, A. (1986) *Leadership and Organizations*. London, Routledge and Kegan Paul.

Burrell, G. (1992) Back to the future: time and organization. In M. Reed and M. Hughes (eds), *Rethinking Organizations*. London, Sage.

References

Cadwallader, G. (1966) The cybernetic analysis of change in complex social organisations. In A. G. Smith (ed.), *Communication and Culture*. London, Holt, Rinehart and Winston.

Child, J. (1982) *Lost Managers*. Cambridge, Cambridge University Press.

Connor, S. (1989) *Postmodernist Culture: An Introduction to Theories of the Contemporary*. Oxford, Basil Blackwell.

Corporate Anthology Foundation (1991) *Newsletter*, 1.

Coser, L. (1956) *The Functions of Social Conflict*. London, Routledge and Kegan Paul.

Dahrendorf, R. (1959) *Class and Class Conflict in Industrial Society*. London, Routledge and Kegan Paul.

Deal, T. E. and Kennedy, A. A. (1982) *Corporate Cultures*. Reading, MA, Addison-Wesley.

Delbridge, R. and Turnbull, P. (1992) Human resource maximization: the management of labour under just-in-time manufacturing systems. In P. Blyton and P. Turnbull (eds), *Reassessing Human Resource Management*. London, Sage.

du Gay, P. (1991) Enterprise culture and the ideology of excellence, *New Formations*, 13(45), 45–61.

du Gay, P. and Salaman, G. (1990) *Enterprise Culture and the Search for 'Excellence'*. Paper presented at the Employment Research Unit, Cardiff Business School Annual Conference, Cardiff.

Earl, M. J. (ed.) (1983) *Perspectives in Management*. Oxford, Oxford University Press.

Edwardes, M. (1983) *Back from the Brink*. London, Collins.

Etzioni, A. (1961) *The Comparative Analysis of Complex Organisations*. Glencoe, IL, Free Press.

Fairclough, N. (1989) *Language and Power*. London, Longman.

Fox, A. (1966) *Industrial Sociology and Industrial Relations*. London, HMSO.

Fuller, L. and Smith, V. (1991) Consumers' reports: management by customers in a changing economy, *Work, Employment and Society*, 5(1), 1–16.

Gellner, E. (1992) *Reason and Culture: The Historic Role of Rationality and Rationalism*. Oxford, Blackwell.

Gergen, K. (1992) Organization theory in the postmodern era. In M. Reed and M. Hughes (eds), *Rethinking Organizations*. London, Sage.

Geuss, R. (1981) *The Idea of a Critical Theory: Habermas and the Frankfurt School*. Cambridge, Cambridge University Press.

Goldthorpe, J. H., Lockwood, D., Bechofer, F. and Platt, J. (1968) *The Affluent Worker: Industrial Attitudes and Behaviour*. London, Cambridge University Press.

Gowler, D. and Legge, K. (1986) Personnel and paradigms: four perspectives on the future, *Industrial Relations Journal*, 17(3).

Guest, D. E. (1990) Human resource management and the American dream, *Journal of Management Studies*, 27(4), 377–97.

Guest, D. E. (1992) Right enough to be dangerously wrong: an analysis of the 'In search of excellence' phenomenon. In G. Salaman (ed.), *Human Resource Strategies*. London, Sage.

Halmos, P. (1965) *The Faith of the Counsellors*. London, Constable.

Hampden-Turner, C. (1990) *Corporate Culture*. London, Hutchinson.

Handy, C. (1985) *Understanding Organisations*. London, Penguin.

Hitt, M. A. and Ireland, R. D. (1987) Peters and Waterman revisited: the unended quest for excellence, *Academy of Management Executive*, 1(91), 91–8.

Hofstede, G. (1980) *Culture's Consequences*. Beverley Hills, CA, Sage.

Hopfl, H. J. (1991) *The 'Corpse' in the Deconstruction of Culture: Some Observations on Dissonant Experience and its Treatment in Organisational Life*. SCOS Conference, Copenhagen.

Hopfl, H. J. (1993) Culture and commitment: British Airways. In D. Gowler, K. Legge and C. Clegg (eds), *Case Studies in Organizational Behaviour and Human Resource Management*. London, Paul Chapman.

Jackall, R. (1988) *Moral Mazes: The World of Corporate Managers*. Oxford, Oxford University Press.

Jameson, F. (1991) *Postmodernism or, the Cultural Logic of Late Capitalism*. London, Verso.

Kanter, R. M. (1985) *The Change Masters*. New York, Simon and Schuster.

Keenoy, T. (1990) HRM: rhetoric, reality and contradiction, *International Journal of Human Resource Management*, 1(3), 363–84.

Keenoy, T. and Anthony, P. D. (1992) HRM: metaphor, meaning and morality. In P. Blyton and P. Turnbull (eds), *Reassessing Human Resource Management*. London, Sage.

Kerfoot, D. and Knights, D. (1992) Planning for personnel – human resource management reconsidered, *Journal of Management Studies*, 29(5), 651–67.

Kinnie, N. (1989) Human resources management and changes in management control systems. In J. Storey (ed.), *New Perspectives on Human Resource Management*. London, Routledge.

Kipnis, D. (1976) *The Powerholders*. Chicago, University of Chicago.

Kotter, J. P. (1982) *The General Managers*. New York, Free Press.

Kotter, J. P. and Heskett, J. L. (1992) *Corporate Culture and Performance*. New York, Free Press.

Lee, R. and Lawrence, P. (1985) *Organizational Behaviour: Politics at Work*. London, Hutchinson.

Legge, K. (1989) HRM: a critical analysis. In J. Storey (ed.), *New Perspectives on Human Resource Management*. London, Routledge.

References

Lewin, K. (1953) Studies in Group Decision. In D. Cartwright and A. Zander (eds), *Group Dynamics*. New York, Row Peterson.

Likert, R. (1961) *New Patterns of Management*. New York, McGraw-Hill.

Louis, M. (1983) Organizations as culture-bearing milieux. In L. Pondy, P. Frost, G. Morgan and T. Dandridge (eds), *Organizational Symbolism*. Greenwich, CT, JAI Press.

MacIntyre, A. (1981) *After Virtue: A Study in Moral Theory*. London, Duckworth.

Mangham, I. L. (1987) *Organisations as Theatre*. New York, Wiley.

Maslow, A. H. (1943) A theory of human motivation, *Psychological Review*, 50, 370–96.

McGregor, D. (1960) *The Human Side of Enterprise*. New York, McGraw-Hill.

Meek, L. M. (1992) Organizational culture: origins and weaknesses. In G. Salaman (ed.), *Human Resource Strategies*. London, Sage.

Morgan, G. (1986) *Images of Organization*. London, Sage.

Mulder, M. (1966) Illegitimacy of power and positiveness of attitude towards the power person, *Human Relations*, 19(1), 21–37.

Ogbonna, E. (1992) Organisation culture and human resource management: dilemmas and contradictions. In P. Blyton and P. Turnbull (eds), *Reassessing Human Resource Management*. London, Sage.

Ogbonna, E. and Wilkinson, B. (1990) Corporate strategy and corporate culture: the view from the checkout, *Personnel Review*, 19(4), 9–15.

Peters, T. and Waterman, R. H. (1982) *In Search of Excellence*. New York, Harper and Row.

Pettigrew, A. (1985) *The Awakening Giant: Continuity and Change at ICI*. Oxford, Blackwell.

Pondy, L. R. (1983) The role of metaphors and myths in organization. In L. Pondy, P. Frost, G. Morgan and T. Dandridge (eds), *Organizational Symbolism*. Greenwich, CT, JAI Press.

Popper, K. (1945) *The Open Society and its Enemies*. London, Routledge and Kegan Paul.

Purcell, J. (1989) The impact of corporate strategy on human resource management. In J. Storey (ed.), *New Perspectives on Human Resource Management*. London, Routledge.

Redfield, R. (1960) *The Little Community and Peasant Society and Culture*. Toronto, University of Chicago Press.

Reed, M. (1989) *The Sociology of Management*. Hemel Hempstead, Harvester Wheatsheaf.

Reed, M. (1992) *The Sociology of Organizations*. Hemel Hempstead, Harvester Wheatsheaf.

Reed, M. and Hughes, M. (eds) (1992) *Rethinking Organization*. London, Sage.

Ricoeur, P. (1984) *Time and Narrative*. Chicago, University of Chicago Press.

Sadler, P. (1988) *Managerial Leadership in the Post-Industrial Society*. Aldershot, Gower.

Salaman, G. (1992) *Human Resource Strategies*. London, Sage.

Salaman, G. and Thompson, P. (eds) (1980) *Control and Ideology in Organizations*. Milton Keynes, Open University Press.

Schein, E. H. (1985) *Organizational Culture and Leadership*. San Fransisco, Jossey-Bass.

Smiles, S. (1908) *Self Help*. London, John Murray.

Smircich, L. (1985) Is the concept of culture a paradigm for understanding organizations and ourselves? In P. Frost *et al.* (eds), *Organizational Culture*. London, Sage.

Smith, C., Child, J. and Rowlinson, M. (1990) *Reshaping Work: The Cadbury Experience*. Cambridge, Cambridge University Press.

Smith, P. B. and Peterson, M. E. (1988) *Leadership, Organization and Culture*. London, Sage.

Starkey, A. and McKinlay, P. (1988) *Organizational Innovation*. Avebury, Avebury Publishing.

Stewart, R. (1967) *Managers and their Jobs*. London, Macmillan.

Stewart, R. (1985) Managerial Behaviour. In M. Earl (ed.), *Perspectives on Management*. Oxford, Oxford University Press.

Storey, J. (ed.) (1989) *New Perspectives on Human Resource Management*. London, Routledge.

Storey, J. and Sisson, K. (1989) *Looking to the Future*. In J. Storey (ed.), *New Perspectives on Human Resource Management*. London, Routledge.

Taylor, F. W. (1911) *Scientific Management*. New York, Harper and Row.

Trilling, L. (1974) *Sincerity and Authenticity*. London, Oxford University Press.

Trist, E. and Bamforth, K. (1951) Some special and psychological consequences of the longwall method of coal-getting, *Human Relations*, 4(1), 3–38.

Turner, B. (1971) *Exploring the Industrial Sub-culture*. London, Macmillan.

Turner, B. (1992) The symbolic understanding of organizations. In M. Reed and M. Hughes (eds), *Rethinking Organizations*. London, Sage.

Unsworth, B. (1992) *Sacred Hunger*. London, Hamish Hamilton.

Williams, A., Dobson, P. and Walters, M. (1989) *Changing Culture: New Organizational Approaches*. London, IPM.

Wilson, D. C. And Rosenfeld, R. M. (1990) *Managing Organisations*. London, McGraw Hill.

Zuboff, S. (1988) *In the Age of the Smart Machine*. New York, Basic Books.

INDEX

Index

Virgin Atlantic, 14
vision, 9

Waterman, R., 15, 16, 81
Weber, M., 38
Williams, A., 43, 89

Wilson, D., 21, 22, 97

Xerox, 42

Zuboff, S., 101